Praise for *Listen Up!*

I think it's first rate. It's very pragmatic. It has useful information in all the chapters and it's the kind of book I would want our managers and people dealing with customers to read.

—Les White
City Manager, San Jose, California

Listen Up! is a classic on the basics of communication that should be required reading for everyone who works!

—Bill Jensen
Author of *Simplicity* and *What Is Your Life's Work?*

I think it is great! Communication is one of the most important elements in business, and one that is not emphasized nearly enough in many work places. *Listen Up!* keeps the reader's interest and has really good advice (some I plan to use in my workplace right away)!

—Sheila Nemec
Supervising Accountant IV

Effective listening is absolutely essential for successful decision making and working together. *Listen Up!* and buy this book for yourself and your co-workers.

—Don Maruska, Master Certified Coach
Author of *How Great Decisions Get Made*

As a speech communications instructor, I consistently place a high emphasis on listening skills. Similar to the style of the classic 1983 book, *The One Minute Manager,* this book is comprised of easy to digest, bite-sized tidbits of information outlining the necessary components needed to achieve effective communication.

—Bill Frisch
Instructor, Monterey Peninsula College, California

I've learned a great deal from this exceedingly well-written book and plan to use it as an ongoing reference guide.

—John Hoover, Ph.D.
Author of *How to Work for an Idiot*

Listen Up! provides a practical set of tools to help people work better together. Although most of us probably think we already know how to listen well, the authors remind us how much more effective we can be by paying attention to this oft-overlooked skill.

—Robin Hall
Human Resources Director

It is an interesting book, comprehensive, and well researched.

—John Culleton
Wexford Press

LISTEN UP!

How to
Communicate
Effectively
at Work

I know you believe you understand

what you think I said.

But I am not sure you realize

that what you heard is not what I meant!

(Anonymous)

LISTEN UP!

How to Communicate Effectively at Work

EUNICE LEMAY &
JANE SCHWAMBERGER

Papilio
Publishing
Soquel,
California

Papilio
Publishing
Soquel,
California

Listen Up! How to Communicate Effectively at Work
Copyright © 2007 by Eunice LeMay and Jane Schwamberger

Requests for information should be addressed to:
Papilio Publishing, P.O. Box 4197, Santa Cruz, CA 95063-4197
www.papiliopublishing.com

Publisher's Cataloging-in-Publication Data

LeMay, Eunice
  Listen up!: how to communicate effectively at work/
  Eunice LeMay & Jane Schwamberger—1st edition.
      p. cm.
  Includes bibliographical references and index.
  ISBN-13: 978-0-9788058-5-2 (pbk.)
  ISBN-10: 0-9788058-5-2 (pbk.)
  Library of Congress Control Number 2006931820
  1. Business Communication. 2. Communication in
  organizations. 3. Listening.
  I. Schwamberger, Jane. II Title.

HF5718.L46 2007
658.4'52—dc22

Printed in the United States of America

Cover Design by Cathi Stevenson, Book Cover Express,
            www.bookcoverexpress.com
Interior Design by Desta Garrett, *dg ink*, dg@dg-ink.net

A Word from the Authors

Why did we write a book on communication in the workplace when there are already a large number of books available on this topic?

Because, based on our past work experience and what we hear from so many in the workforce, it's our conviction that there's *still* a need for *improved communication* on the job! When we began to write this book our research uncovered that many, many books have been written on the subject of the lack of communication in business, some going back to the 1970s. Some of the books were written by academics and were boring. Many publications failed to convey to management just how *much* poor communication negatively impacts a company's bottom line. Others dealt with only one aspect of communication, and so on.

The question that kept haunting us was: Why, then, with all of these books on the subject, are companies and organizations *still* experiencing such a high degree of *a failure to communicate*?

The conclusion we came to is that the problem is not so much a failure to communicate as it is *a failure to LISTEN*! Lack of effective listening has impeded our collective ability to effectively communicate.

Both of us have worked as employees and in management. As a Library Director in Florida, Jane practiced a highly successful communication program. Eunice experienced nothing but poor communication until we met as Training Librarian and Assistant in a California library. Our research and our personal workplace experiences as boss, employee, and co-worker have enabled us to assemble the proven, workable techniques presented in this book that can be learned and used by *everyone*. We know we have finally found the key to how to achieve success in communicating *effectively* at work.

So *"Listen Up!"* And let this book show you how to find success as well!

Our own experiences (which includes our combined *sixty* years at assorted workplaces including banks, insurance companies, classrooms, nursing homes, publishing companies, factories, fast food restaurants, computer software companies, retail stores, and libraries) proved to us that the need for better communication is endemic in companies both large and small. In our search through past writings about communication in general, and workplace communication in particular, we did find much that is of value and in need of incorporating here.

- Our goal is that this book will consolidate in one place the basic communication skills *you need* to know to successfully communicate at work.

- Our intention is that it will provide the essentials you need to successfully communicate with bosses, co-workers, and customers.

- Our aim was to make it brief, but to the point. It is our hope that the Index, Table of Contents, and layout will make it easy to find useful information *you and your company need* to achieve successful communication within the whole organization.

And, in the end, we hope that you, our readers, will tell us we have succeeded because *Listen Up!* taught you *How to Communicate Effectively at Work.*

Eunice LeMay

Jane Schwamberger

Contents

Part Two—Effective *Communicating*

PART THREE—"Utopia, Inc." and You!

APPENDIX

Foreword

Most people would assume that communicating verbally is fifty percent listening and fifty percent speaking. However, upon conducting an in-depth examination of what it takes to produce high-quality, effective communication it becomes clear that developing the ability to actively listen with the intent to gain understanding reveals that listening may well be seventy to eighty percent of the communication equation. We've been given two ears and one mouth for a reason!

Listen Up! is all about listening with a purpose; and that purpose is to facilitate effective communication. Eunice LeMay and Jane Schwamberger have done a masterful job at examining the listening process and developing key techniques to help you learn how to communicate more effectively. The Listening and Communicating Tips provided at the end of each chapter provide a blueprint for effectively understanding content being shared in order to respond in a meaningful way. Putting yourself in your "listener's shoes" is a particularly useful exercise to improve communication both verbally and in writing. We particularly appreciate the research the authors did to gather knowledge from multiple sources to help you learn how to *Listen Up!*

You can never convince someone you care unless you are willing to *Listen Up!*

—James & Bond Wetherbe
Consultants, lecturers, and authors of
So, What's Your Point?

PART ONE

Effective *Listening*

Listening Is the Key

"I have no idea what is going on—I only work here!"

"Nobody ever tells me anything."

"Nobody ever listens to *me!*"

Have you heard such statements where you work? Have you said them yourself?

We certainly have. *Lack of communication* is one of the top ten complaints of both employees and management. The most common complaints among employees include:

- Not understanding what is going on

- Not knowing what is expected of them

- Not being asked for input on work directly affecting them

It is well documented that the type of management style that results in such unhappiness is, in fact, *bad* for the bottom line. When there is little or no communication within an organization, productivity and morale suffer, while absenteeism and costly staff turnover increase. But this does not need to be the case. Good communication skills can be *learned*. Developing an

effective communication system within an organization is not
difficult to implement. It simply requires determination and a
bit of work. And the rewards are far greater than the energy
expended to accomplish it.

What Is Effective Communication?

Communication can be defined as a dialogue between two
or more people that results in a mutual understanding. Other
definitions include the sharing of information and also the meeting of minds to achieve agreement. Our definition of effective
communication is:

> *Information that is exchanged clearly and concisely,*
> *so that true understanding has successfully occurred.*

Perhaps some examples of poor communication will make
the point. The following are actual management comments taken
from John Hoover's book, *How to Work for an Idiot* (212):

- "Teamwork is a lot of people doing what I say."

- "This project is so important, we can't let more
  important things interfere with it."

- "E-mail is not to be used to pass on information or data.
  It should be used only for company business."

- "We know communication is a problem, but the company
  is not going to discuss it with the employees."

Why Is There Such Poor Communication?

There are several possible reasons why so many companies
have failed for so many years to foster good communication
within their organizations. In the 1970s many organizations had
management and CEOs who were men from a generation that

is sometimes called the "Silent Generation." They more than likely had served in the military during World War II or Korea, and were comfortable following the military-style hierarchy in organizations, where orders were issued and they were obeyed. There was no thought given to discussion with the rank and file or solicitation of their input for decision making.

In more recent times, it could be argued that the workplace has become more culturally diverse and thus suffers from a lack of understanding of these cultural differences. These differences influence how people react to what they hear from bosses, co-workers, and customers. This makes effective communication even more of a challenge.

One could also argue that historically there has been an antagonistic relationship between workers and management. This has either created the need for unions, or, in some cases, the unions have exacerbated this tension (depending on your point of view). It has also been said that the rank and file have the power to disempower management, and to thwart whatever goals management is trying to achieve. These views are usually based on the belief that management and the rank and file members have very different goals, and that each is trying to get the most out of the other with the least degree of reciprocal effort. Therefore, so the argument goes, it is in neither one's best interest to listen to the other side, nor to try to work together toward a common goal.

Still others believe that management in general has no idea what is going on in an organization or how to accomplish a given goal, therefore, how can they be expected to communicate accurate and useful information to those whom they manage? It is true that people are often promoted to management positions without getting proper management training and, therefore, they cannot communicate efficiently and effectively with those they manage.

Is Anybody Listening?

However, we believe that the most compelling explanation for this lack of communication in business is that NOBODY IS LISTENING! We are all too busy talking. We are so bombarded with information that we have tuned it out. We are so caught up in our own busy lives and concerns and the minutia of daily life that we are not listening to what others have to say. Since only fifteen percent of our brain is needed to process the words that our ears are hearing, the other eighty-five percent of our brain is busy with other things. This makes it impossible to do active listening. We are not processing and evaluating and trying to *understand* what the person speaking to us is really trying to say.

The Benefits of Good Communication

Our experiences and our research have shown that many benefits result when there is effective communication in the workplace. The primary ones are reduced stress and greater cooperation. There is also more time and less frustration, since clearer instructions inevitably reduce the amount of rework. There is less tension and greater cooperation among employees and management when there is a better understanding of each other, a clearer understanding of their assigned duties and resulting expectations, and a realization of how everyone is working together toward a shared goal. For employers this creates greater productivity and an improved bottom line. For the employees it means that difficult people (customers, co-workers) can be successfully dealt with, and tasks can be implemented with the least amount of effort and hassle.

Most of this is accomplished by eliminating the *misunderstandings* that arise from poor communication. In *So, What's Your Point?* James and Bond Wetherbe report that *eighty percent* of the problems at work and in relationships are not problems per se, but misunderstandings. If we don't *understand* each other, it is impossible to be efficient and productive in our jobs. The Wetherbes (*Preface*, xi) sum it up well: "Perhaps the single most important skill a person can develop is the ability to communicate effectively with others. Only through effective interpersonal communication can one persuasively convey an idea, overcome objections, avoid misunderstandings, and minimize arguments."

You Can Achieve Success!

This book will cover these essential points:

- How to listen effectively

- How to talk and write well

- How to deal with difficult people

- How to improve communication within the whole organization

The book is divided into three parts. In Part One you will learn about effective listening. Part Two will show you hands-on techniques for turning what you have learned into successful communicating. It will also deal with specific aspects of communication from the perspectives of management, the employee, and the co-worker and/or customer. Finally, Part Three will give you a perfect example of effective listening and communicating, and show you how to turn what you have learned into reality in your daily work life.

You will learn how to improve your verbal communication—both some general ideas and specific items such as how to do presentations and run meetings in Chapter 9. You will find out about how different genders and age brackets communicate in Chapter 4. Also, you will learn how to write well—especially e-mail—in Chapter 10.

And if you prefer concrete examples to general theory or instruction, Chapter 13 will show you how a company called "Utopia, Inc." practices effective communication.

A Win-Win Situation

The rewards for establishing an atmosphere where effective communication is the norm results in a *win-win* situation for all involved—employees feel valued and appreciated; the company becomes highly productive and avoids costly absenteeism and turnover.

Even in the absence of any policy or practice of effective communication within your organization, you can still practice what is suggested in this book and thereby improve your own workplace atmosphere. Stress and tension will be reduced and life will look and feel better. It can be done. Whether you are a "small fry" or a "big cheese," you can make life better for yourself, and others, by becoming a more effective communicator.

For those who are skeptics, we say: "What have you got to lose?" *If what you and/or your company is doing today is not working, why keep doing it?* Read on, and learn how you, too, can achieve success.

Let's get started!

1

Active Listening

You're Not Listening! Pay Attention!

Our ability to be good listeners is one of the most important and unrealized aspects of effective communication. Communication implies a dialogue between two (or more) people—one talking and the other(s) listening.

Three Types of Listening

Allan Glatthorn and Herbert Adams, in their book, *Listening Your Way to Management Success* (1–3), break down listening into three types—Hearing, Analyzing, and Empathizing. We were not born with these skills, but they are skills that can be learned. To paraphrase Glatthorn and Adams:

1. *Hearing* is receiving the words that are spoken. This is what we usually think of when we talk about listening. It focuses on the literal meaning of what was said.

2. *Analyzing* involves determining what the purpose or true *meaning* of the words are. It requires the listener to actively analyze the words, and use critical judgment to understand what is really going on. It takes more work to think about what it all means.

3. *Empathizing* is the most complex type of listening. The listener must be fully *present* to what the speaker is saying, and respond in a supportive and accepting way. The listener must *hear* what was said as well as what was left *unsaid*. The focus here is on the person, not the words spoken.

Blocks to Effective Listening

Glatthorn and Adams (7) point out that there are many things that will prevent us from hearing what someone has to say. Being aware of some of them will help you to find ways around the blocks and therefore facilitate more effective listening. For instance, as a listener, you may:

- Be distracted by a lot of noise and/or activity in the room.
- Be wrapped up in yourself and your own concerns.
- Have a personal animosity toward the speaker.
- Be unfamiliar with the technical terms or jargon being used.
- Be unable to process what you have heard, i.e., it has virtually gone in one ear and out the other.

Active Listening Techniques

Listening is an active pursuit which is both hard work and demanding. One *cannot* be a passive listener *and* a good listener. The following are techniques all of us can use to improve our listening skills:

- Focus all your attention on the speaker.
- Set aside your prejudices and opinions.
- Listen to the very end.
- Do not formulate a response in your head while the speaker is still talking.

- Compare what is being said with what you already know. Is it valid?
- Listen for feelings and observe body language and tone of voice to better assure understanding.
- Ask for clarification to increase understanding.
- Restate or paraphrase to verify your understanding.

Jotting notes while someone is speaking is one way to allow you to concentrate on the speaker and still remember your questions or comments when they have finished speaking.

The most important thing to remember when listening to someone is to practice active listening:

- Examine what you are *hearing* against what you know.
- Evaluate any evidence in *support* of what is being said.
- Separate statements of *fact* from opinions, suggestions, recommendations.
- *Summarize* and, if you can, categorize what you are hearing.

Then, when it is *your* turn to speak, *first* pick up on something that was just said and use that as a hook or transition to what you are going to say. This shows that you *were* listening and also that you found some value in what you just heard.

Asking Questions and Rephrasing

One of the keys to good listening is the ability to ask good questions. Questions should be open-ended, meaning they require more than a simple "Yes" or "No" answer. Questions should be specific to the immediate issue or current problem and not vague and general. "What is the problem?" is not as helpful as asking, "What exactly is preventing you from completing this project on time?" Asking questions can work well with a complaining customer or a difficult co-worker as well as a supervisor/manager. It helps to clarify the problem as well as reinforce that you are both on the same page.

To assure that you both understand each other, it is also a good practice to rephrase or paraphrase back to the other person what you *think* he or she is saying. You can either rephrase it in the form of a question, or make a statement and then ask, "Is that correct?" or "Am I understanding that correctly?"

As James and Bond Wetherbe (62) explain, "Here is a quick review of the four reasons why the rephrase is important:

1. To validate the communication;

2. To create an agreeable mind set;

3. To force yourself to listen; and

4. To allow yourself more time to formulate an answer. . . .

Whether you *think* you've understood or *not*, rephrase to be sure." In any situation, it is always helpful to paraphrase back to the speaker what you think you heard him say, so that any misunderstanding can be quickly cleared up.

Active Listening Keys

Let's summarize the three keys to active listening presented above:

1. *Focusing on the speaker and listening respectfully* until the speaker is finished.

2. *Listening actively* and *interpreting* what is being said to you.

3. *Asking clarifying questions* and *providing feedback* to assure you are in agreement with the person speaking.

A Quick Test: How Active a Listener Are You?

Imagine the following conversation:

> "Sally, we have received a complaint that you are not very friendly when talking to a customer on the telephone. The customer making the complaint felt that you were giving her scripted answers and not letting her fully explain the problem."
>
> "What do you mean I'm not friendly? I'm as friendly as anyone here."
>
> "Well, the customer said you interrupted her and didn't seem to care about helping her with her problem."
>
> "You only give us five minutes per call. Some people will go on and on about their problems."
>
> "Look here Sally, I don't want to hear your excuses. Just be more friendly when you talk to the customers. I don't want to have to deal with any more complaints."

Now, look up from this page and interpret (or repeat) in your mind what you have just "heard."

Checklist for Active Listening

Check your active listening ability by asking yourself these questions:

- What exactly was the nature of the customer's complaint? What specifically did Sally do or say to the customer that got the customer upset?

- Are the employees given possible or sample answers to certain problems?

- Was there just the one complaint? How has Sally performed before this?

- How realistic do you think a five-minute time limit per call is for most problems?

- How do you interpret the final statements of Sally's supervisor?

Next, re-read the original conversation.

Now, pick up on some aspect of what was being said and use it as a starting point to ask a question or clarify a particular aspect.

Listening actively or attentively is not easy, as you may have just found out. You need to do more than just process the words spoken. You will need to analyze what was said and what the speaker meant to say. Then you need to make sure that you truly did understand (using questions or paraphrasing) what the speaker was trying to say. This does take some work, but with practice can be done quickly and successfully. The benefits are well worth the trouble.

Three Things to Improve Your Active Listening

What might you do the next time to improve your active listening skills? Here are three sample questions:

1. How might you improve your ability to focus on the speaker?

2. How would you go about interpreting what is being said?

3. How can you be sure that you and the person speaking are in agreement?

Now, think of three things *you* can do to improve your active listening.

Summary

Listening attentively will save you time in the long run. If you put aside all distractions and focus on the person speaking, you will avoid misunderstandings. If you are a supervising manager or the instructing co-worker, you will not have to repeat yourself. If you are the employee or the listening co-worker, the activity will not have to be redone because you were not listening to, or did not understand, the instructions.

Remember, practice makes perfect. Start to model the behaviors you want others to emulate. If you begin to listen attentively to them, they will be more likely to listen to you!

Listening Tip #1:

Listen Attentively!

If you are listening attentively, you will discern what other people have said and you will be able to tailor your response to fit *their* needs—as well as *yours*.

Motivating Your Listener

Why Should Anyone Listen to You?

Equally important to our ability to listen is our ability to get the other person to *want* to listen to us! This is not always easy. We are all busy or distracted with our own concerns. In this chapter and the next, we will discuss motivating skills which are part of the essential skills employees and management must develop to improve the effectiveness of their own communication.

How do you get others to both *listen* and *talk* to you? You will need to stimulate interest in others to *listen* to what you have to say. To do that requires you to understand their needs, their "hot buttons," and their interests in order to reach out to them. You will also need to determine their workplace behavior type and their preferred way of learning/communicating. This information can then be used to motivate them to *listen* to you.

Getting to Know Your Listener

The best way to communicate with anyone is to take time to think about the person, or persons, you are talking to. Try to determine their perspective, point of view, or interests. Then appeal to that while making your point, i.e., if the person is interested in sports, use sports metaphors to make your point. If what you say can hit one of your listener's "hot buttons," you have given him a compelling reason for listening. The best way to find out what a listener's interests or "hot buttons" are is to listen to what *they* are saying. Talk to them. Ask them. At some point they will give you clues in their conversations. Then ask yourself: *"Why should they listen to me?"* The challenge is getting them to *want* to listen.

This is particularly important because many of us have very short attention spans. As we have mentioned, it takes only fifteen percent of our brain to process what we are hearing. That means eighty-five percent of most people's brains can be wandering around, daydreaming, thinking about dinner, or the ball game after work, or anything else it might want to do. More often than not, it does not include listening to you!

There are a number of different ways that people can be grouped, including behavior types, personality types, and learning types. These groupings all show how different some people can be and how they require different approaches to deal with them. The following section presents one way to group people by different workplace behavior types.

Who Are You Talking To?
Three Workplace Behavior Types

Research done by psychology professor, David C. McClelland, shows there are three very different behavior types with very different work and management styles. These distinctively different work and management styles are based on what motivates them to act as they do. They include:

1. Those who value what society or others believe is proper behavior or a definition of success;

2. Those who are "anti-players" that defy or resist society's plan for them;

3. Those who follow their own internal beliefs or voices.

Based on these three motivating factors, McClelland classified them in his book, *Human Motivation* (595–598), as Affiliation, Power, and Achievement. (Sonya Hamlin, in her book *How to Talk So People Listen* (13), refers to them as Affiliators, Influencers, and Achievers.) McClelland's classifications can be described as:

1. **Affiliation**—Affiliators need to affiliate with others or be included in a group. They are friendly and want to be liked and to help others. This desire to be included tends to make them conciliators when there is conflict. They prefer to work in group projects, teams, or committees. In fact, few businesses can run successfully without some Affiliators in their employ.

2. **Power**—Influencers want to have the power and authority to direct others or influence them. They have a need to exert control. They can be good team leaders or managers, if they can motivate others to work toward a stated goal.

3. **Achievement**—Achievers are self-motivated and work hard to achieve personal success. They enjoy competition and challenges but do not always work well with others. They strive for excellence and meaningful work. Most entrepreneurs are Achievers, but they do not necessarily make good managers. They prefer to work alone. They are great problem solvers. They need to get feedback and appreciation for their work.

If you can understand these differences in what people want and how they act on those wants at work, you can come up with a method for dealing with them. Learning to deal with all three types and what drives them will result in effective communication with them.

For example, you might tell the *Affiliator* that you would be happy if she would work with you toward a solution for your problem. You would ask the (*Power*) *Influencer* for help in getting the *team* to work toward a solution or make him a team leader. And you might appeal to the *Achiever* to help find a solution to the problem. As a memory hook, you can remember the songs that Sonya Hamlin (14–19) associated with the three types:

Affiliators—*People Who Need People,*

(Power) Influencers—*They Did It My Way,* and

Achievers—*Climb Every Mountain.*

Let's See How It's Done

Start here by making up a problem or think of a real problem you have encountered. Then pick one of the behavior types above and think about how you would phrase the question or request—according to what you think would be the most effective way to motivate that person to listen to you. If it is helpful, you may wish to identify colleagues in your workplace who fit the categories described and then imagine posing your request to them.

Now, let *us* try it.

A. Here is an example:

You work in the Accounting Department and it is budget time. You need to submit a detailed budget projection for next year.

B. Here is the kind of *help* you need:

You need a team to collect the cost figures, print up a report, and present it to the Board of Directors in a PowerPoint presentation.

C. Here are the three ways you can phrase that request:

1. (To the Affiliator) Will you be part of the budget team and help collate the cost figures?

2. (To the Power-Influencer) We need you to assemble a team and get them working on the budget figures. Can you do that?

3. (To the Achiever) Would you take the budget figures and make a PowerPoint presentation that can be presented to the Board of Directors?

D. Here is the *information* you need:

Detailed figures for each department from the department heads.

E. Here are the three ways you can ask for that information:

1. (From the Affiliator) We are gathering the budget figures from all the department heads. We would really appreciate it if you can get yours to us by next week. Will you be able to get it done by then?

2. (From the Power-Influencer) Can you get your people working on the budget figures? We will need them by next week. Can your people handle that?

3. (From the Achiever) Will you have your budget figures decided on by next week?

Summary

The failure to communicate in the workplace is not inevitable. It can be changed. Each one of us can start by taking responsibility for making sure that we understand others, and by making the effort to motivate others to *want* to listen to what we have to say. We do this by respecting their individual workplace behavior types.

LISTENING TIP #2:

Motivate Others to *Listen* to You by *Listening* to Them.

As James and Bond Wetherbe state (165):

"Understanding other people's perspectives so you can address their concerns, manage their expectations, overcome objections, and avoid misunderstandings is mutually beneficial, not manipulative. *Communicating effectively results in win-win situations.*" [Emphasis ours.]

Listen to Learn

Learn People's Learning Preference

Usually what you need from a co-worker, manager, or employee is information or help. As discussed in the last chapter, the first thing required is to get to know the person you are asking so that they will *listen* to you and be able to respond to your request.

You do this by determining what *workplace behavior type* they are, and what will motivate them to listen to you. If you are able to determine the behavior type of your listener, you will be able to determine the best way to approach that person. In like fashion, once you have determined your *own* behavior type, you will be in a better position to let others know how they can communicate most effectively with you!

It is interesting to note that the "Myers-Briggs indicators" have sixteen personality and work styles. (See the Bibliography at the back of this book if you wish to investigate these personality types further.) In addition to the three workplace behavior types—Affiliators, Power-Influencers, and Achievers—discussed in Chapter 2, there is also another standard of grouping people into four personality groups—Relaters, Initiators, Analyzers, and Drivers. However, be aware that the validity of personality groups for use in defining individuals in the workplace is being questioned. Annie Murphy Paul is one of those questioning using personality types to define workplace groups. For more information on this, see her book, *The Cult of Personality*, listed in the Bibliography. For more detail in handling various behavior types, as opposed to personality types, with specific suggestions if such a person is your supervisor, your co-worker, or your employee, see the newly revised and expanded book, *Working with Difficult People*, by Muriel Solomon.

The Three Learning Types

In addition to different behavior types, there are three differing ways of learning—Visual, Auditory, or Kinesthetic (hands-on). Understanding the type of learner you are speaking to, and also knowing the type of learner *you* are, will be of great benefit. You can determine what type of learner you are dealing with by listening to and observing them.

Visual learners prefer written instructions and will say to you: "I don't *see* what you have in mind," or "What I am *looking* for is . . . ." For such learners, you could hand them written instructions of what is needed, or actually show them how something works or how something should look (so that they are visually engaged).

The *Auditory learner* will listen to verbal instructions and say to you, "Can you *tell* me what you have in mind?" or "I *heard* you say you wanted. . . ." They may ask you a question—even when a written example is right in front of them. For such learners it is best to talk directly to them, explaining what you need, and/or by verbally giving them instructions.

Kinesthetic learners are "hands-on" learners who will use their own hands to shape and describe objects. They prefer to do things themselves rather than read about it or be shown how to do it. They generally prefer maps and diagrams. They will use words like *build, move,* or *get.* For them it is best to guide and help them in *doing* something, but not to demonstrate it for them. You could say to them, "I'll walk you through it the first time so you will know how to *do* it."

You can then use these same techniques when asking each of them follow-up or closure questions: "Do you *see*? Do you *hear* what I am saying? Do you *understand*?" and also, "Is there anything else I can *show* you, *tell* you about, *help* you with?"

Now ask yourself, "What is *my* preferred way of learning?" And now, think about a couple of your co-workers and see if you can determine which would be their way of learning.

Respect for Our Differences

Beyond learning behavior types and learning preferences, it is imperative that you treat your co-workers with courtesy and respect. This may not always be easy, especially when there is conflict. In conflict situations, it may be helpful to view dealing with your colleagues as performing *internal customer service.* This can help you to establish a more amicable relationship with them. "Do unto others as you would want them to do unto you." Think about what your alternative is. Do you want to work with tension, strife, and stress? An efficient and smooth running office is worth the time and effort to establish good communication and cooperation.

Summary

Developing and practicing the skills we've presented in Chapters 2 and 3 will result in:

• *Understanding another person's viewpoint and what motivates them* to listen to what you have to say;

• *Understanding different workplace behavior types* and how to communicate most effectively with each one;

• *Understanding the different ways people learn* and tailoring your message to the other person's preferred way of learning/communicating;

• *Relating to co-workers with respect* and appreciation for their individual uniqueness.

Listening Tip #3:

Listen to Discover How People Learn.

Listen to learn what a person's learning preference is and you will know whether you need to communicate with them in writing, verbally, or through "hands-on" interaction.

Blocks to Effective Listening

Viva the Diversity in the Workplace!

Whether it is nature or nurture that influences our communication style, we can all learn to communicate more effectively and forcefully. Realizing, understanding, and respecting our many differences will help us achieve that goal. It is helpful for all of us to become aware of how the words we choose can have a negative impact upon our listeners, as well as convey impressions of strength or weakness.

Gender Differences

There are a number of popular books that claim there are basic, innate differences between men and women besides the obvious sex differences. Among other things, they point to the differences between how men and women communicate. It is important to be aware of these differences. In many instances women choose words that give the impression of weakness instead of selecting powerful action words. Phyllis Mindell in her book, *How to Say It for Women* (22–27), talks about how using "I" statements (and the "touchy-feely" emotional verbs that go with them) make women appear childlike. Using emotional words along with the "I" word makes any individual seem immature, tentative, and unprofessional. But using powerful action words will show strength and compel others to listen.

One reason many women are not getting promotions may be due to the way they communicate. In the last decade or two we have heard the term "glass ceiling" (a barrier based on attitudinal bias) used to explain this lack of promotion. It was thought that women don't have what it takes to be leaders. They are thought to be soft and weak, not strong and powerful enough to deal with all the problems entailed in running a large organization or department. While we now can point to a number of women who have proven that idea to be incorrect, it is still an issue when a woman is being considered for promotion.

Rosalind Barnett and Caryl Rivers, in their recent book *Same Differences*, state that communication differences are the result of the power positions that men and women often hold. Until recently, women have been in the subservient position and so acted accordingly. As women are gaining higher positions of power and are supervising men, it is the lower ranking men who are now showing subservient behaviors, including the ways in which they communicate.

Anyone, whether man or woman, can learn to use words to communicate strength and competence and, therefore, be listened to.

Cultural Differences

We also fail to communicate due to assumptions we make about other people. We might assume they are hostile to us, or they are different from us and so will not understand, or that they are too slow, or not as well educated, or too highly educated, or that they do not share our same values, and a host of other negative internal messages.

Some of this faulty thinking has come about because often there are great cultural differences between individuals at work. Many cultures have different ideas on personal space. Many traditional Asian women feel they would be showing disrespect if they look a speaker in the eye. Businesses and schools are accommodating Muslims' need for prayer times throughout the day, which might interfere with a timeline or deadline. People from some cultures will always say "Yes" first to be polite, even if the real answer is "No." Some prefer Mr. and Mrs. or Ms.— while others use first names or abbreviate even the first names! Understanding all these differences can be difficult.

Generational Differences

Another important consideration when trying to understand co-workers is generational differences. We now have four very different generational groups working together (and some may say "clashing") in our stressful, competitive workplaces. (Lynne Lancaster and David Stillman, in their book, *When Generations Collide,* explore in depth this clash between the different generations.) Therefore, you cannot assume that the employees gathering around the water cooler have the same life experiences or cultural touchstones. This can create communication challenges that can only be dealt with by understanding their differences. These generational groupings explain the ways in which their upbringing during different historical eras affects their views and how they respond or react in various situations, problems, or assigned tasks:

- *Silent Generation or Traditionalists:* Born in the 1920s to 1940s, these individuals experienced two world wars and the Great Depression. They are generally stable, loyal, and hard working but change does not come easy to them. With the war background many of them had, they believe in and are used to what Lancaster and Stillman (20) call the "chain of command" style of management.

- *Baby Boomers:* Born 1945–1960, they experienced prosperity, moving to the suburbs, and TV. They include the first large group of working moms. They are idealistic and service oriented, but not good at feedback or compliments. They were going to change the world and make it a better place, so you might say that they believed in what Lancaster and Stillman (22) refer to as "change of command." By the sheer volume of their numbers, they became very competitive for each position in the corporate world.

- *Generation Xers:* These include the first latch-key kids (born 1960–1980), and they are usually independent, impatient, cynical, and techies influenced by the great technology boom. They often have poor people skills. They are bright and hard working, but believe in a balance between their work and personal life. Their skepticism prevents them from having the kind of loyalty to a company that the Traditionalists have. They do not have the competitive drive of the Boomers, but expect their intelligence and hard work will result in promotions up the corporate ladder. Being independent, Lancaster and Stillman (26) would say they believe in "self-command."

- *Generation Y or Nexters or Millennial Group* (1980–2000): These people grew up with the Internet and so were exposed at an early age to the universe. They are usually viewed as smart, tenacious, pragmatic, and are good at multitasking. They are good at dealing with difficult people and have excellent group skills. You could say, as Lancaster and Stillman (31) do, they believe in "don't command—collaborate!"

Summary

The workplace today includes a very diverse group of people. Not only do we have gender and cultural diversity, but we also now have generational differences that affect how we view work, and how we interact.

Listening Tip #4:

Realize, Understand, and Respect Individual Differences!

Choose words that will have a positive impact on your listener.

5

What Your Listener Sees and Hears

Using Body Language, Tone, and Attitude Effectively

Why is body language important? James and Bond Wetherbe assert that you can dramatically increase your impact by developing appropriate non-verbal communication skills. Communication experts tell us that only seven percent of the meaning of a verbal communication comes from the actual words, while thirty-eight percent comes from the tone of voice, and fifty-five percent comes from body language! A listener will look to the speaker's body language to either confirm or contradict the words that are being said.

What Is Body Language?

Body language involves:

- Facial expression
- Body posture or stance
- Hand gestures
- Eye contact
- Proximity (boundaries/personal space)
- Physical contact (touch)

BODY LANGUAGE QUIZZES

Try the following two quizzes taken from James and Bond Wetherbe's book (100–102, used by permission) and see if you can "hear" the communication conveyed through body language.

BODY LANGUAGE MATCH QUIZ

First, study the three examples of someone talking on the telephone, and based on his body language, determine who he is portraying. Then, match each with a, b, or c below.

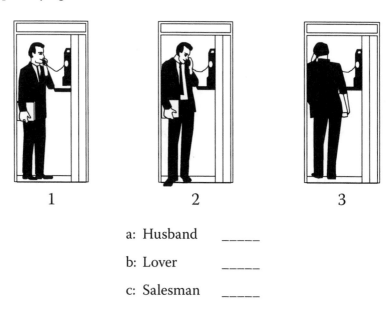

a: Husband   _____

b: Lover   _____

c: Salesman   _____

OK, let's see if your impression matches what was intended.

Picture 1 is the *salesman*. He's saying, "All right, I'll get that shipment to you next week."

Picture 2 is the *husband*. He's standing rather relaxed saying, "OK, you want me to pick up a carton of milk, a loaf of bread, and what else?"

Picture 3 is the *lover*. He's whispering, "I can hardly wait! I'll meet you tonight at 8:00."

Body language can *say* a lot!

The next body language quiz is a little more difficult because you have limited information—no movement, no facial expression, no sound—just a silhouette. Study each one before reading further.

Silhouette Match Quiz

Try to match each silhouette (1 through 6) with the label (a: through f:) listed below:

a: Openness, looking for acceptance ____	d: Headache ____
b: Relaxed negativism ____	e: Closed acceptance, defiance ____
c: Lecturing ____	f: Aggressiveness ____

Now let's see how well you did. Some of these are tricky because the differences are very subtle.

Openness is silhouette 5. Her arms are in an open, accepting position with palms facing forward and upward.

Relaxed negativism is silhouette 4. Arms are crossed and he is leaning slightly backwards.

Lecturing is silhouette 1. By the way, finger pointing is generally not a good practice.

Headache is silhouette 3. I'll bet you got this one correct.

Closed acceptance is silhouette 2. This one is easy to confuse with aggressiveness. The difference is in the width of the stance and the placement of the hands on the hips.

Aggressiveness is silhouette 6. Hands on the hips and a wide stance indicates that this person is ready to do battle.

Body language messages *do* communicate.

What is a listener "hearing" from *your* body language?

Tips for Effective Body Language

The non-verbal communication of your body language can say more than the words you are using. Experts estimate that ninety percent of our message isn't what we say, it's how we say it. Remember, too, that non-verbal communication varies from culture to culture. The following suggestions reflect U.S. culture:

- Eye contact is important, particularly when you are listening.

- Body language can be used to indicate interest in what the other person is saying.

- Avoid hyperactive gestures such as foot or pencil tapping, or jiggling knees, keys, or coins.

- Nodding occasionally as a person talks encourages him or her to continue.

- Facial expressions can be used to communicate compassion, empathy, and interest.

- Proximity is a cultural variable. If a person backs away, you are probably too close.

- Touching is a touchy issue. Some people don't like it. When in doubt, don't.

Summary

Make eye contact, smile, and use open-handed gestures while you talk. You will be perceived as being friendly, honest, open, and caring. The easiest way to convey positive body language is to *be* open, honest, caring, confident, and enthusiastic about your subject. These positive traits will be conveyed (without your having to think about them) to your audience.

Listening Tip #5:

Listen to the Non-verbal Communication.

A listener will look to the speaker's body language to either confirm or contradict the words that are being said. Positive gestures will convey that you are listening—or communicating—empathetically, with a true desire to understand or to be understood.

Review

Before proceeding to Part Two, let's review
the *Listening Tips* discussed in Part One:

Listening Tip #1:   *Listen* Attentively.

Listening Tip #2:   Motivate Others to
                         Listen to You by
                         Listening to Them.

Listening Tip #3:   *Listen* to Discover
                         How People Learn.

Listening Tip #4:   Realize, Understand,
                         and Respect
                         Individual Differences.

Listening Tip #5:   *Listen* to the
                         Non-verbal
                         Communication.

PART TWO

Effective *Communicating*

6

Techniques for Effective Communicating

For most of us, the majority of our communication involves one-on-one interactions. The other person we are communicating with may be a customer, co-worker, or supervisor. In all cases, the same skills can be used to successfully and effectively communicate.

Speak Assertively

We often fail to communicate due to fear—fear of being judged negatively, or being laughed at, or appearing stupid, or not being able to control our emotions, or saying the wrong thing. But these fears can be overcome by developing self-confidence and learning to control our emotions. If you don't yet have these traits, act as if you do. You will be surprised at how quickly they will surface. Self-confidence will help you speak assertively when you need something or are trying to resolve a problem.

Think Before You Speak

Of course, before saying anything, you should stop and *think*. Think about:

- *Who* are you talking with?

- What is their learning *type, age, interests?*
- What would *motivate* them to *listen* to what you have to say?
- What do you *want* to say?
- How can you say it *clearly* and *concisely?*
- Do you have any preconceived ideas or prejudices that will taint an open and honest discussion?
- Can you keep your emotions under control?

Use the Active Voice

Let's look at powerful ways to communicate. The most effective way is using active verbs instead of passive verbs. This means *subject-verb-object.* It is called the "active voice" because the subject "acts out" the verb. In the passive voice, the verb is passive. An example of each is:

- "The report was written." (passive)
- "The manager wrote the report." (active)

When the passive voice is used it is often unclear as to who is doing the action. This can lead to misunderstandings and a lack of clear communication. Take the example of this sentence from Phyllis Mindell's book, *How to Say It for Women* (40): "A solution should be found for this pressing personnel issue." Four managers were asked to recast the sentence into the active voice and each came up with a different name or title of who should find the solution. No wonder we often have situations where no one knows who does what in a company!

Be Concise

Many people feel overworked and stressed. One way to save time is to be clear, concise, and to the point in your communications. Also, strive to never have to repeat yourself. Always focus on the problem or task to be done. Do not get sidetracked by irrelevant issues or personality differences. Always respect the person you are talking with, even if that person is being difficult.

A great example of how to do this is found in the book, *The One Minute Manager,* by Kenneth Blanchard and Spencer Johnson. They believe that anything you have to say can be said in one minute or less. So take a moment to organize your thoughts before you start to speak. Think about the person you are talking to. Where are they coming from? What is their perspective? What motivates them? What self-interest of theirs can you appeal to? Namely, "What is in it for *them*?" Then take another moment to ask yourself, "What do I want to communicate to this person and how can I say it in one minute or less?"

One model that may help you focus on the key, essential points when communicating can be found in the book entitled, *The Simplicity Survival Handbook,* by Bill Jensen (28):

". . . In a hurried, get-it-done-now workplace, most everyone wants every communicator to:

- Get to the point! What's the one thing you want me to remember? *(Know)*

- Show me you care about my needs. *(Feel)*

- Be clear about what I'm supposed to do next. *(Do)*

Know, Feel, Do is a concise preparation tool for communicating in any morebetterfaster environment."

It is, then, just a matter of practicing repeatedly this clear and concise way of speaking until it becomes a habit. You might try practicing being concise when writing e-mail. Take time to think through what you want to say and how you can say it in as few words as possible. It might also help to enlist some friends who will let you practice saying things clearly and concisely. The time you save by not having to repeat yourself, re-explain something, or redo mistakes will more than make up for the time you will need to learn how to speak concisely.

Thinking versus Feeling

Although we don't agree with this, one school of thought indicates you should start conversations with an expression of how or what you are feeling, particularly when you are having a problem with the other person. Starting a conversation with, "I feel frustrated when you come back late from lunch," *is* better than saying, "You are always late getting back from lunch!" In such cases, "I" statements are better than "you" statements (i.e., "I feel your comments are offensive" is better than "You are a jerk!").

A popular notion in the '70s was that we all should express our feelings and not hold anything in. This may be a good idea for personal and family relationships, but it does not make for good work relationships. The reason is that the main focus at work for everyone is *how to get the job done.*

Therefore, rule number one is: Get rid of "I" statements or "feeling" words at work whenever possible. Phyllis Mindell (40) tells us: "Verbs that can inject emotions into professional language include 'feel,' 'like,' 'don't like,' 'want,' 'need,' and others that convey emotion rather than action: just the kind of language women are accused of using." These words do not convey strength and confidence, which is what companies are looking for in leadership positions.

Another school of thought says that it is better to say "I *think* we need to talk about this problem." Again, "I *feel* that is a bad proposal" might sound better as, "I *think* that is a bad proposal."

Avoid "I" Statements

Still another school of thought says forget the "I" words alto-gether. Be inclusive and use "we" when appropriate, as in "*We need to talk.*" Start your conversation by pointing out areas of common interest or concern. It puts you on the same team as your listener instead of in an adversarial relationship. And, again, use action words instead, or use the active voice.

Remember: *You are at work to get a job done.*

Concentrate on that and not on your feelings. "That is a bad proposal" may work best of all.

Emotional versus Powerful Wording

Let's look at some examples that show the difference between emotional wording and powerful wording:

Emotional   *I like your idea for a minority outreach grant.*

Powerful   This minority outreach grant will increase attendance in our new reading program.

Emotional   *Our committee likes the idea of training staff to do stretching exercises. We feel it would be beneficial.*

Powerful   Training staff to break and stretch will reduce workplace injuries. Our committee supports this proposal.

Emotional   *Bill, it was very nice having lunch with you,* or *I was happy we had the chance to have lunch.*

Powerful   Bill, our lunch meeting produced many good ideas.

With a little bit of practice, speaking powerfully will become a valuable tool for communicating more effectively at work.

Trim Hedges

A second weak language form is hedging. To hedge, according to Phyllis Mindell (30–32), is to "hide behind words, refuse to commit oneself." People who use these statements sound as if they doubt their own words and lack authority. Phyllis Mindell gives examples:

> "You shouldn't do that, really. . . .
>
> Well. . . .
>
> I'd like to get the promotion, sort of. . . .
>
> In my opinion. . . .
>
> The way I see it. . . .
>
> I guess. . . .
>
> I just. . . .
>
> I would like to. . . .

In addition, some hedges belittle you:

> I'm not sure how strongly I feel about this, but. . . .
>
> I guess my question is. . . .
>
> I'm not an expert on that, but. . . .
>
> I would like to. . . .
>
> I may not be right, but. . . ."

When there is genuine uncertainty, Phyllis Mindell (32) suggests "Words like *might, may, can, should, promises, seems to,* and *appears to*" can be used without appearing weak.

(Note also how many of the above phrases begin with the word "I.")

Slash Modifiers

Another problem with clear, strong communication is vague modifiers. Note how clear the sentence is when you are more precise. The following examples will clarify this point:

Vague modifier	*It's really very important to respond to the alarm.*
Precise	Not responding to the alarm will result in injuries.
Vague	*Many of the students were late.*
Precise	Half of the class arrived ten minutes late.

Too Many Words

Phyllis Mindell (31–32) says women have been accused of talking too much, but studies have shown that men both talk and *interrupt* more than women! We all are guilty of using more words than are necessary to communicate effectively and efficiently. The same points just discussed can also be used to cut wordiness. Let's review them:

- Avoid "I" statements.

- Trim hedges.

- Use the active voice.

- Slash modifiers.

Say No Powerfully but Kindly

Most workers today, regardless of gender, culture, age, or other variables still don't have powerful or effective ways of saying "No." Using the active voice as discussed earlier will certainly help. Phyllis Mindell (251) suggests ways to "say no without seeming hostile, mean, or aggressive:

Ten Ways to Say No Powerfully

1. Perhaps a better solution is available.

2. That solution doesn't promise success.

3. That solution doesn't sound practical.

4. This solution promises to be more economical.

5. Time won't permit this meeting to continue.

6. This problem deserves attention. Let's set up an appointment to do it justice.

7. Company policy prohibits gifts from vendors, but thank you.

8. Rather, consider this alternative.

9. The data don't support this conclusion.

10. This conclusion seems to be based on inadequate data."

Summary

The way to effective communication is to:

- Think before speaking.

- Choose powerful, precise language using action verbs.

- Make your point clearly and concisely.

- Then stop.

Communicating Tip #1:

Choose Words That Convey Strength and Confidence.

7

Dealing with Problem People

Conflict Resolution with Customers and Clients

Most jobs today involve delivering some kind of service to customers. Whether conducting business in person or on the telephone, it entails verbal communication. Customer service is finding out what the customer's needs or wants are, and then giving it to him. It is important to understand your customers' wants, needs, thoughts, and feelings, and what will satisfy them so they will return. The following are ten basic human needs from *Quality Customer Service* by William B. Martin (42), that "reflect the needs of your customers or clients.

1. The need to feel welcome.

2. The need for timely service.

3. The need to feel comfortable.

4. The need for orderly service.

5. The need to be understood.

6. The need to receive help or assistance.

7. The need to feel important.

8. The need to be appreciated.

9. The need to be recognized or remembered.

10. The need for respect."

One way to remember these ten needs is to remember to treat people as you would like to be treated. In other words, deal with customers with respect, courtesy, tact, and calm.

Listening Is Very Important

In order to know what the customer's specific needs and wants are, it is important to listen. This entails applying the active listening skills discussed in Chapter 1. It is particularly important to listen carefully when the customer is not particularly skilled at communicating their needs and/or wants. Then it is important to ask clarifying questions, to listen actively to the responses to the questions, and to repeat back to the customer your understanding of what you just heard. Once you have agreement as to what the customer wants or needs, provide him with a solution (if at all possible) that will satisfy him.

It is also important to listen to what his body language is saying in order to understand what his needs and wants are. Then look for clues as to the best method for fulfilling his needs and wants. As discussed in Chapter 3, there are three different models for the way that people learn new things—visual, auditory, or kinesthetic (hands-on). When trying to communicate new information or explain something to customers, you will be more successful if you can determine which method works best for each customer. You can determine this by looking for clues in both their body language and what they say.

Communicating Effectively

The following are some general do's and don'ts for effective customer service:

- Greet customers with a smile when they approach. Stop talking to co-workers or doing other tasks.

- Make eye contact unless you think their culture believes that is insulting.

- Give them your full attention.

- Listen carefully to understand their wants and needs.

- Ask open-ended or clarifying questions to determine their needs and wants.

- Rephrase to ensure that you fully understand their wants or needs.

- Whatever it may be, if possible, if you have the power, give them what they want.

- If you cannot give them what they want, offer alternatives. Ask them "What would satisfy you?" or "What would you like?"

- End with some type of closure comment to leave the customer feeling appreciated, satisfied, and wanting to return.

Sometimes good customer service involves written communication such as letters or e-mail. The same communication skills and rules apply. This is also true when dealing with a customer over the phone. Always smile. It will be reflected in your tone of voice. Also, remember that cultural differences may come into play. When in doubt as to what to do, ask the customer or client. Then rephrase to assure understanding. This is especially effective when dealing with a conflict situation. As James and Bond

Wetherbe (58) state: "If there is one time that it is important to understand correctly what someone is saying and what someone means, it is when they are starting to get upset—a conflict situation."

Angry Customers

People often become angry when they are under a lot of stress. Our society today seems to be forever in a hurry and our work responsibilities seem to keep growing. This creates more and more stress in our lives. Life has become so stressful that "free-floating" frustration is common. Our fast-paced society has made us accustomed to instant gratification. Daily stress and high expectations lead to frustration when anything moves slowly or goes wrong. All employees in service positions have to deal with this. Sometimes, the company or institution may really have an unrealistic or inefficient policy that is frustrating both clients and staff. Some clients may want more service, but don't want to pay for it. In other words, they may want something you cannot provide.

The Librarian's Way

Librarians have a technique they call the "Reference Interview." They ask open-ended questions to try to ascertain what exactly their customers want in the way of information. This saves them a lot of time they would have spent getting the wrong or incomplete information. It also results in customers getting precisely the information that they need. It involves simply asking questions, and maybe even repeating back to customers what they understand them to be saying, until both the customer and the librarian agree about the information needed.

"Give 'em the Pickle"

Even if it is not your standard procedure to give a client or customer what they want, it may be worthwhile to do so. Bob Farrell, owner of Farrell's Ice Cream Parlours, coined the phrase "Give 'em the pickle." When a customer wants something —for instance extra pickles with his sandwich—then it is worth the cost of a few pickles to keep the customer satisfied, willing, and eager to come back. That phrase has come to symbolize the concept of doing those special or extra things that are important to satisfy customers. Whenever you can, "Give 'em the pickle."

Of course, we realize in some organizations "Give 'em the pickle" is not a possible choice. If you are employed in transportation, government, or law enforcement, there will be times when this won't work. These organizations demand that certain rules be followed explicitly for safety reasons.

In situations where the customer is angry, you can begin with an apology. Apologizing does not mean you are wrong or the organization is at fault. You can say you are sorry that the person is upset, angry, or has been inconvenienced. You can also agree with the customer when they are correct on some point without conceding the whole discussion.

Lack of effective communication can lead to people assuming the bully role. Customers push and insist they get what they want, rather than having a calm discussion on what can be done to accommodate their needs. When they take on the bully role, you end up being the victim of their rants. You do not have to take verbal abuse from your customers—whether external or internal (your co-workers). You can take control of the situation and defuse the anger and/or pushiness. The hardest thing may be to not react defensively and not to take personally anything that is said. Keep the focus on the issues and away from egos.

Look for areas of agreement and build on those. As James and Bond Wetherbe (75) state: "When dealing with difficult people, be sure not to lose your cool by telling the other person that he or she is being a jerk. Just keep asking questions in a helpful and constructive manner. . . . Phrase your questions in a tone and manner of wanting to help or understand."

The Four-Pronged Approach to Effective Customer Service

Sometimes customers just want to vent. Let them. Then ask them what they would like you to do for them. The following is a list of four steps to deal with angry people which can also be used to resolve any conflict situation:

1. If the person is angry, let them vent or let them say what they need to say. Focus and show them you are listening to what they have to say.

2. When they are through talking, paraphrase back what they said, minus the anger. For example:
   "If I understand you correctly. . . ."

3. If you have a remedy for the problem, then propose it—quickly.

4. If you cannot come up with a satisfactory solution, ask the other person: "How would you like to resolve this?" or "What would satisfy you?"

It may not be possible to give the person what he or she wants. In that case:

- State what you can do for them, not what you cannot do.

- Give them some options that they can choose from.

- Try to never use the word "No."

> • Say instead, "That would go against our stated policy. What I can do for you is. . . ."

Listening Is the Key

We cannot emphasize enough the importance of being a good listener! Understand the customer's point of view. Understand that it is not personal. She is not trying to be difficult. She may be under stress, and/or very frustrated. Deal with the problem or situation, not the behavior. Do not deal with the personality or consider the person as the problem. Use non-trigger words like "Tell me more."

The following are some good statements that can be a bridge to move the conversation to resolution:

"How can I help you?"

"I can help you with that."

"Here's what we can do."

"What do you want me to do for you?"

"What will satisfy you?"

"Thank you for bringing this to our attention."

Troublesome or Dangerous Customers

People who deal with the public may, on occasion, have to deal with a person they suspect may be on drugs, inebriated, or acting inappropriately. Deal with them the same way you would with any other customer unless they are disruptive or pose a danger to themselves or others. In those instances, inform them that their behavior is unacceptable—"I'm sorry, but your behavior is unacceptable in this store."—and inform them that if they continue they will be asked to leave. If they don't stop the unacceptable behavior, call the security department or the police and have them removed from the premises.

The same approach applies when on the telephone. If a caller is swearing, tell the caller that use of such language is unacceptable. State that you will not continue the conversation if the behavior is not stopped. If it continues, warn the caller that you are going to hang up now and then hang up the phone.

As an employee, know when to pass the problem on to your supervisor. If you do not have the power to give the customer what he or she wants, or if you are unsuccessful in satisfying his or her needs or wants, refer them to your supervisor. They may have more flexibility in what they can do for the customer. Ideally, this should be a rare occurrence. Staff should be empowered to handle the most common situations that may come up.

When you are the supervisor, try not to undermine your staff's previous efforts by giving in to a pushy or angry customer, especially after an employee has just insisted that what the customer wants cannot be done. Make it clear to your staff which rules can be bent to satisfy a customer and which are firm. If you feel you need to bend or break a rule, explain to the customer that you're making a "one-time" exemption to the rule. Another response would be to assure the customer that you will change the policy so it never happens again, but only if he has brought to your attention a policy that needs changing. [NOTE: Most supervisors can't change company rules but they can pass suggestions on to those who can.]

If, as a supervisor, you do give in to the customer, explain to your staff why you did it. Employees need validation that they did the right thing. Explain how you would like a situation like this handled in the future. And when you tell them they were correct in how they handled it, tell them sometimes exceptions need to be made and it's your job as supervisor or manager to do that.

Conflict Guidelines

The following four steps are good general guidelines to follow for any conflict or customer service situation:

1. Listen to what the customer is saying.

2. Acknowledge any sign of frustration or anger.

3. Ask clarifying questions to assure you understand.

4. Offer a solution or alternative options.

Summary

The keys to effective customer service are:

• Give the customer or client your full attention.

• Listen to the speaker for clues that will aid in understanding that person and what he or she is trying to say.

• Look to body language to enhance that understanding.

• Ask clarifying questions and offer solutions or alternative options.

• Try to give them what they want or need. Ask them, "What would satisfy you?"

Put another way:

• Smile.

• Care.

• And, "Give 'em the pickle!"

Communicating Tip #2:

Practice
"Customer Service" with
Everyone You Deal With.

Everyone needs to feel welcome, understood, appreciated, and respected.

8

Dealing with Problem People

Conflict Resolution with Co-Workers

When there are disagreements or conflicts with co-workers or between a supervisor and employee, it is more important than ever to have effective communication skills. The previous chapter gave some tips on dealing with difficult customers. The same methods will work with co-workers. Probably the best approach to apply is known as the FIRR technique:

Facts. Start the conversation by stating the facts (not your feelings). *"What exactly is the problem?"*

Impact. Explain how the problem or their behavior is affecting you or the situation. *"What are the consequences?"*

Respect. Since you will have to continue to work with this person, it is very important to try to maintain a good, respectful relationship.

Request. Ask for what you want, or for the reasonable outcome you want to achieve.

Generally, it is better to leave *feelings* out of any discussions at work. It may be appropriate to mention feelings under the

FIRR "Impact" step (page 59), because the impact may be that the problem behavior or situation is making you angry, frustrated, impatient, or crazy. In that case, it is OK to state how you feel. Just remember to do it in a respectful way.

Remember the Librarian's Way

Remember our discussion of the "Librarian's Way" in Chapter 7. A librarian, interacting with a customer at a library's Reference or Information Desk, might ask "Could you be more specific?" or "Would you explain that in more detail?" or "What kind of information about _____ are you looking for?" This provides the librarian with a much clearer picture of the complexity or depth of information that is required and, in the end, makes for a satisfied customer. If you are not a librarian, you can still emphasize this technique. Asking questions can work well with a difficult co-worker or a manager who doesn't tell you what is going on.

When you do get cooperation or assistance from a co-worker, remember to express appreciation for their help. It only takes those two little words, "Thank You!"

Dealing with Negative and Resistant Co-Workers

In nearly every workplace there are one or more persons who will not respond in a positive way to your direct, respectful approach. Negativity can be defined as anger, complaining, resentment, passive-aggressive behavior, resistance and/or interpersonal conflict. Negativity can also be contagious. It can spread from one negative person to the whole group, department, or office. A complainer, for instance, can stir up the whole group or cause resentment or anger against a person or situation.

There are a number of ways that negativism can manifest itself in the workplace. Some obvious negative behaviors include:

- unfriendliness

- complaining

- defensiveness

- lack of humor

- procrastination

Behavior can range from one extreme (passive) to the other (aggressive). The norm or preferred middle ground can be called "Assertive." Dealing with people in an Assertive manner entails three traits:

1. Directness

2. Honesty

3. Respect

Dealing *directly* with someone means talking to the person who is exhibiting the negative behavior. It does not mean complaining to anyone and everyone about the negative person or situation. It also doesn't mean complaining to anyone above you in management. That should be done only if the direct approach is unsuccessful.

Dealing *honestly* with someone means telling them clearly what you perceive to be the problem and how it is affecting you and/or others.

Dealing *respectfully* means respecting the thoughts, feelings, and perspective of the person with whom you are speaking. This is often the hardest to do when negative attitudes or behaviors are involved. But it is very necessary if there is to be a successful resolution of the problem.

When attempting to discuss a person's skepticism, the approach used is absolutely critical. Correct, non-confrontational communication skills are required to reduce the other person's taking a defensive stance. An important first step is examining the *intent* of the communication with that person. Do you want to vent? Do you want to put him in his place? Or do you genuinely want to work with her to find a solution you can both live with? When you do approach the person, use phrases such as, "Your negative reaction to every idea that is brought up in staff meetings is unhelpful." After stating the problem and how it is impacting you, or the office staff, or productivity in general, propose a "partnership of understanding." This involves listening (respectfully) to the other person's view of the situation, then paraphrasing (not parroting) back what was said until you both understand each other. This may help you to understand that the other person may have a different, but legitimate, view of the situation. Then, and only then, both participants in the discussion can explore possible solutions. If this process fails, then tell the person that you will approach the appropriate management level person to act as mediator in further discussions.

Another aspect of approaching the discussion with the right attitude is to not assume that the negative person has some conscious evil behavioral intent. This person may not even be aware of how skeptical they appear. Such negativism may have been so ingrained since early childhood that the individual may not be aware of any other way to behave. So you could possibly be doing them, and their co-workers, a favor by informing them how their behavior is adversely affecting others.

Responding to Negativity

However, be prepared for responding statements about *your* negative traits! Acknowledging that they may have a point, if they do, and then being the first to offer to make some changes in your own behavior, may more readily elicit positive offers of change on their part.

Since negativity is contagious, it is always helpful for all of us to examine our own behavior and look for evidence of negativity in ourselves. Is another person's procrastination or resistance causing you frustration? Do you find yourself complaining a lot about this person instead of approaching the person directly? We must be aware of our own negative behaviors before we can change them. Try to remain positive. Remember the cliché— "When life gives you lemons, make lemonade." Just as negativism is contagious, so, too, is a positive attitude. You can help lift the cloud of skepticism in your workplace by looking for the positive.

The Bottom Line

The bottom line is that you cannot change other people. You can try to influence them or ask for their support, but you cannot force them to change their behavior. Like the proverbial horse, you can lead them to water but you cannot make them drink. The only thing you have control over is how *you* respond to people or situations. If all efforts at understanding and working with the other person fail, you will need to decide what you are going to do. You will have three choices. They are:

1. Keep trying to communicate with them and achieve some understanding.

2. Give up trying and find some way to learn to live with it.

3. Find employment elsewhere.

Always attempt to talk to the negative or difficult person respectfully in hopes that the person will be willing to discuss the issue. If that fails, attempt to get your manager or department head to deal with the situation or person. Your third choice is to decide if you can live with the situation or if you will need to leave this workplace. Do you love your job and only have to deal with this person occasionally or is the situation intolerable? You must weigh the positives and negatives and then decide what to do.

If you practice using the effective communication skills discussed in this book, more often than not, you will be able to resolve differences and enjoy good relationships with your colleagues. The chance of success is definitely worth giving it a try.

Summary

Use the FIRR technique to resolve conflict:

- State the *Facts*.
- Explain the *Impact* or consequences.
- *Respect* the person.
- *Request* the outcome you want to achieve.

Deal with people directly, honestly, and respectfully.

Communicating Tip #3:

When There Is a Problem, Deal Directly with That Person.

Since negativity is contagious, counter it with a positive attitude, which is also contagious.

9

Verbal Communication

Even though it may seem that we are doing most of our communicating through e-mail, we continue to do a lot of communicating verbally. We still go to many meetings, attend classes, or give demonstrations, and have discussions in the hallway. However, a good deal of business is still conducted by telephone and the telephone continues to be an efficient method for business communication in the workplace. Lengthy (or any back and forth) discussion is better handled via the telephone than by e-mail. Communication is more than just words. People listening to you must also interpret what you are saying to determine just what you mean. They will be able to interpret some of your meaning by your tone of voice. But when you are on the telephone, the other person will not be able to use visual clues, such as body language, to interpret your message. Therefore, it is more important than ever that you say exactly what you mean—that you speak clearly, concisely, and to the point.

Telephone and Voicemail Guidelines

Practice all the communication skills discussed earlier (e.g., asking questions, listening attentively, and thinking before you speak). It is important to think carefully about the words you will use since they will be your only means of communication besides tone of voice. If you're fearful you'll forget something you need to convey, write down what you want to say. When making what you think will be a challenging call, write out in detail some useful phrases to use. Following are some guidelines: [NOTE: Company policies may vary.]

Format/Rules/Troubleshooting for Telephone

- Always answer the call promptly, preferably by the second or third ring.

- Identify yourself (department name, your name) when you answer a business phone.

- Smile and sit tall. It conveys respect to the caller.

- Other than taking notes, do not engage in other activities (eating, drinking, shuffling papers) while on the telephone.

- If you have to keep someone waiting on hold for any length of time, apologize for the delay.

- Conclude your call with "good-bye."

- Always return calls promptly.

- Avoid listening in on co-workers' telephone conversations or making comments about them.

- It is discourteous to hang around a co-worker's

desk waiting for the conclusion of his/her phone conversation. Leave and come back again later.

- When using a speakerphone, be discreet and always consider the privacy of the caller.

- Whenever using a cellular phone, keep your voice low and don't disturb others.

Format/Rules/Troubleshooting for Voicemail

The following are some guidelines for better voicemail messages:

- Always keep your outgoing message up-to-date, especially if you're often away from your desk for an extended period of time.

- If you are going to be away for a period of time, it is helpful to let callers know when you expect to return and to provide the name of another person they can call for assistance.

- When you are the caller, briefly explain your reason for calling so the person called will know how to respond when they return your call.

- When leaving a message, always speak clearly and spell difficult names. When leaving your phone number and/or e-mail address, speak slowly. It is also good to let the person know when would be a good time to call you back.

- If your voicemail allows for this, indicate to the caller the length of a message they can leave. You could indicate in your voicemail, " . . . Leave a detailed message" or, if your caller will be cut off after one minute, ". . . Leave a brief message."

Presentations and Demonstrations

Presentations can be said to be a one-on-one conversation—only with a whole room full of ones you are conversing with! It can be a one-sided conversation, if you do not get feedback until the end or until a question and answer period. (However, you might get feedback in the form of body language such as people falling asleep, looking at their watches frequently, yawning a lot, or tapping their feet nervously—in which case it would be a good idea to move along quickly.) Because of a lack of feedback as you make your presentation, it is very important that you plan carefully what you want to say and how you want to say it. Doing a presentation with slide after slide of bullet points, and/or reading aloud all of the bullet points, will guarantee to bring on the above-mentioned body language feedback. The following is a chronological checklist to use when preparing a presentation or report:

- Opening—grab the audience's attention with a question, a story, or a provocative statement.

- Engage the audience—tell them why they should *listen* to you—how does it benefit them?

- Overview—tell them what you are going to talk about (and possibly give some background information to show why the topic is important).

- Body
    First key point
        Supporting information or examples
    Second key point
        Supporting information or examples
    Third key point, etc.

- Summary of the speech so far—you cannot state the message too many times.

- Anticipate questions or objections—if you think there may be some, answer them before they can be asked or stated.

- Recap the key points you want them to take away and remember.

- Closer—a call to action. Tell them what you want them to do.

- Question and Answer session—ask if there are any questions.

Organizing your points into a certain order and structure makes it easier for the audience to follow what you are saying, especially in light of today's short attention spans.

If the audience doesn't know you, their first question will be "Who are you?" Therefore, introduce yourself and tell a bit about yourself to establish your authority and credibility on the topic you are presenting. Other good rules to follow include having an attention-getting opening (i.e., a startling fact, a statistic, a very short story, or a subject-related joke). Use short, simple, clear words and sentences. Don't use "insider" language or "business-eze." (For more on this, see Don Watson's book, *Death Sentences: How Clichés, Weasel Words, and Management-Speak Are Strangling Public Language*.)

Pauses or silence can also be used to great effect. When you say something important or ask a rhetorical question, leave a gap after it—a pause. Let it hang there for several seconds. It gives the listener time to think about what you just said. In fact, they cannot help but think about it.

Remember also to speak loud enough so you can be heard in the back of the room.

Using analogies (stories or examples) not only aids in understanding, it reinforces in a way that is memorable and amusing to listen to. The very best way to get a point across is to paint a picture or use words visually so the listener can "see" as well as hear what you are saying. A picture is worth a thousand words. It makes your statements interesting and compelling. Research has shown that we remember eighty-five percent of what we see, and only fifteen percent of what we hear. This may be due to the fact that with TV, movies, videos, DVDs, etc., we have become a visual society. Seeing is believing. It is much easier to remember something if a picture of it exists in our mind. For example, compare these two sentences:

> "We must work together as a team."

> "Ay, we must all hang together, else we
> shall all hang separately." (Ben Franklin)

One final thing: Perfection is overrated. It is OK to fail. Failure is a great teacher. Learn from your mistakes so you can do better the next time. If you want to improve your presentation skills, consider taking a public speaking course or joining a local Toastmasters group. (Local groups can be found at www. toastmasters.org.)

Do's and Don'ts of Meetings

Are meetings really necessary? Maybe you are one of those people who think you could get a lot more work done if you didn't have to attend so many meetings.

Meetings can be important and productive, but too often they waste time and accomplish little. Why should we have meetings? It depends on what you want to achieve. If your purpose is to disseminate information, a memo, fax, or e-mail may do the job just as well or better. However, if you want to gather information or feedback, or want to collaboratively work on solving a problem, then a meeting may be the best way to do it. Just remember there are monetary costs involved (not only the salary paid for the time staff are attending the meeting, but there could also be travel time and transportation charges involved). There is also the time spent preparing for the meeting, which includes making an agenda, and the time spent preparing the minutes after the meeting. There is also the problem of staff being unavailable for other duties while in a meeting.

Why then have meetings? Team-based companies have found that most of their work gets done in meetings—the group dynamics create more energy for projects or goals. They found that meetings are beneficial for the following reasons:

- To brainstorm new ideas or come to a consensus

- To promote buy-in by allowing people to see their role in the big picture

- To establish goals, guidelines, or timelines

- To obtain instant feedback

- To provide unique insights, gather data, sell an idea, or generate alternatives

- To resolve conflicts within or between groups

- To foster in-depth discussions which clarify murky points

Effective Leadership in Meetings

Often meetings don't work because of a failure of leadership. This can result in lack of direction, ineffective exchanges of information, poor listening, or too little participation. There can also be overbearing leadership that can lead to hostility and resistance. Therefore, the following guidelines are recommended:

- Assign a definite timeframe for the meeting so staff will know when they can expect it to begin and end.

- If possible, it's best to distribute the agenda prior to the meeting so that attendees are prepared to contribute to the discussion.

- Arrive early to set up/check out the room to make sure any equipment needed is working.

- Ask for a volunteer to take minutes or assign someone to do so.

- Provide multiple copies of handouts so everyone has a copy.

- The Chair of the meeting must keep control of the meeting.

- The Chair should not dominate the meeting or try to influence the discussion.

- Participation should be encouraged but long-winded talkers should be curtailed.

- Meetings should start on time. Never wait for latecomers and never repeat or recap what the latecomer missed; it is not fair to those who made the effort to arrive on time. Ask the latecomers to take on the responsibility of finding out what they missed.

- It is very important that the person running the meeting stick to the agenda (i.e., finish each agenda item before moving on to the next), take care of business, and adjourn on time.

- Remember, making comments such as, "That's an interesting idea," or "That's an interesting way of looking at it," doesn't mean you agree or need to expand on the suggestion in the discussion.

- When someone interrupts you or another speaker, hold up your hand in the stop signal or hold up your finger as if to say, "Just one minute," and continue or let the speaker continue talking. Or, if need be, say to the interrupter, "Please let me finish . . . (pause). Thank you." Then continue.

- If someone is dominating the discussion, ask for input from someone else by name.

- If others are talking while you are talking, encourage sharing by saying, "I'm glad to see you all have ideas on this. Tom, would you share your thoughts with us?"

- Finally, if something comes up which is not on the agenda, add it at the end and discuss it then, if there is time to do so. Otherwise, schedule it to be dealt with at the next meeting or at some other time.

Summary

The same communication skills for face-to-face exchanges are needed when using the telephone. Keep your outgoing voice-mail message up-to-date. Presentations, demonstrations, and speeches should always have an opening, the main body of information, and a wrap-up restatement of the main points for a conclusion. Sometimes meetings are necessary. Good, effective meetings start on time, stick to the agenda, and adjourn on time.

Communicating Tip #4:

Speak Clearly, Concisely, and to the Point.

Whether talking on the telephone, giving a presentation, or conducting a meeting, ask questions, listen attentively, and think before you speak.

10

Written Communication

$\mathbf{A}$s in verbal communication, certain guidelines apply in written communication. Written communication can be the preferred method if you want to establish a "paper trail." Be very aware of tone in written communication. Without the visual clues in a face-to-face discussion, miscommunication can occur. It can be hard to tell if someone is using sarcasm or trying to be funny. This is the reason e-mail writers frequently add "smiley" faces, "LOL" (laughing out loud), or other descriptive symbols.

Written communication has the advantage of giving you time to think about what you want to say. You can think about the audience, exactly what you want to say, and how to say it clearly and concisely. You can organize your message in a logical, sequential way that will be easy to follow. Business communication also requires a certain formality. Remember to check your punctuation and spelling, which has become easy to do with the Spell Check and Grammar Check features of word processing programs. Although you may prefer written communication, keep your audience in mind and, if you know it, their preferred way of learning/communicating. (See Chapter 3.) For example, prepare written versions of communications for those who learn best by reading. Also, determine what is the best method for the particular piece of information—the content you want to impart to the recipient.

The CLEAR Model

The recipient of any written communication will want to have the following five questions answered, especially if you are asking them to do something. Bill Jensen, in *The Simplicity Survival Handbook: 32 Ways to Do Less and Accomplish More*, (41), calls it the CLEAR model:

"Your communication must convey:

How is this relevant to what I do?	**C**onnection to their workload
What, specifically, should I do?	**L**ist action steps
What do success and failure look like?	**E**xpectations for success
What tools and support are available?	**A**bility to achieve success
WIIFM—What's in it for me?	**R**eturn to that person"

E-mail

Let's start with what has quickly become the number one method of communication—for both business and personal communication—e-mail. It is estimated that 1.3 trillion e-mail messages are sent annually. E-mail tends to be seen as a "quick and dirty" method of correspondence. Because this viewpoint is shared by many individuals in the business world, it is easy to get into trouble when viewing e-mail as ephemeral or short-lived. This is not the case. Your employer has the legal right to read any electronic correspondence created and received on company-owned computers. A survey by the Society for Human Resource Management indicates that nearly sixty-three percent of the companies surveyed monitored e-mail activity. Keep in mind, e-mail does not disappear completely when you press the delete key!

When sending e-mail it is vitally important to fill in the subject line. The subject line should clearly indicate what the message is about. Junk e-mail, or spam, is so prevalent today that many recipients quickly hit the delete button without even reading the message unless convinced of its authenticity and relevance. Filling in the subject line with pertinent information tends to reduce deletions. So include the most important aspect of the message first (identify what you are responding to) to pique the reader's interest. Realize that he may not read the whole e-mail.

When you reply to an e-mail, make sure the reply goes only to those you want to receive the reply and not the whole group that may have received the original message. Consider this also when deciding who needs to receive a copy ("cc") of your e-mail. Decide who in the company needs to get it. Many do not have time to read all the e-mail they get. Send your e-mail only to those who really need the information. On the other hand, it's probably better to err on the side of sending an e-mail to one too many people rather than one too few, which could leave out someone who should really be included.

Netiquette

The second item to review is etiquette—netiquette. The following guidelines apply when writing e-mail, responding to a listserv (messages sent to or received by members who are part of a list), or blog (an on-line journal that is frequently updated) on the Internet:

- Be brief.

- Be respectful. Don't say anything you wouldn't say to a person face-to-face in a room full of people.

- Check spelling and grammar, as with any form of written communication.

- Proofread your message before sending it and make sure all the attachments you want to send are included.

- Use descriptive—but brief—subject headings.

- Remember your audience.

- Limit humor, sarcasm, and the use of "smileys." ☺

- Summarize when responding by quoting the portion of the message you are responding to.

- Give back. If you request information on a listserv and receive many responses, then compile the responses with appropriate editing and post them.

- Don't repeat what has already been said, unless there's a need for consensus.

- Cite references, if you use them to support your assertions.

- Be aware of addresses so that you don't send a private message to the list or send a message to the wrong list.

- Consider responding off-line to save time for listserv participants.

- Forgive others' mistakes and vow not to make them yourself.

Remember, when responding to e-mail:

- If you're going to be away from work for more than a few days, be sure to arrange for your e-mail to send an "Out of the office" reply to those e-mailing you so they don't have to wonder why you haven't gotten back to them.

- Respond to requests made to you via e-mail the way you would to requests made via telephone calls, letters, or memos. It's discourteous to leave people hanging. A simple "I'll take care of it," or "I'm on it," or "I'm not able to attend, but thanks for asking," is all that is needed. Otherwise, senders feel as though they have sent their requests out into space and are left with a feeling of not being communicated with. Err on the side of courtesy. You'd say "Thank you" over the phone or in a letter. Why not with e-mail?

- Never respond immediately to an e-mail that angers you. Instead, write your angry reply but, whatever you do, don't send it! Rather, keep it in your "Drafts" folder. Twenty-four hours later you will want to rewrite it or delete it.

Memos

E-mail is an electronic memo. So follow the recommendations above under e-mail/netiquette.

Letters/Correspondence

- Keep business letters short and to the point.

- Limit your letters to one page whenever possible.

- Emphasize the reader's perspective: "What's in it for me?"

- Avoid beginning too many sentences with I, we, my, or our.

- Limit your sentences to twenty words or less, interspersing shorter sentences with longer sentences.

- Avoid writing in the heat of anger, as you may say things you'll regret later.

- End with an action step that suggests the reader's next move or yours.

- Use correct spelling, punctuation, and grammar. This includes correctly spelling the recipient's name.

Notes

When leaving a note (Post-It or otherwise), remember to legibly sign it and date it. Initials are fine, if they are legible and easily communicate who you are to the recipient.

Reports

As stated earlier, always ask yourself who your audience is:

1. Who will be reading this report?

2. Who will be using the information in the report? If it is for stockholders or investors or will be used for marketing, it should be formal, detailed, and printed on glossy paper. If it is a progress report for in-house management, it may be less formal. It should report the information clearly and concisely.

3. Then ask yourself, what should the report accomplish?

4. What do you want to say?

5. How can you say it clearly and concisely?

6. Follow all the basic rules of written communication mentioned earlier. Headings will help readers get through your report quickly. Numbering paragraphs can be helpful when you need to refer to certain sections during a meeting. It's good practice to ask a co-worker to proofread it—especially for content—before distributing it.

You may need to prepare a summary or outline of the report for those who only need key information.

Minutes

When writing minutes of a meeting, state who was there and what was discussed. Keep minutes brief with enough detail so that those who were not present can understand what was discussed. Include the task assignments. Distribute the minutes to all those who were present as well as any others who need to know what was discussed. You may include everyone in the company if the subject affects them all. It is unfair to expect employees to hit the ground running on something which management has been discussing for some time, but is entirely new for the staff. Therefore, keep employees informed about current activities, meetings, and discussions by sending a copy of the minutes or an e-mail outlining what has transpired.

Whatever you are writing (e-mail, letters, reports, or even short notes) please Spell Check and Grammar Check it and read it carefully before sending it. It is embarrassing and time consuming to correct errors that could have been caught by simply reading what you wrote. Do not assume that the spell and grammar checks will catch everything. Too many words sound alike but have different meanings and spellings.

Signs and Labels

Signs and labels are forms of written communication. Clear and precise signs and labels promote good communication. They are especially important when staff have to share a desk. Drawers at multi-staff use desks should be neatly labeled, allowing staff to quickly find what is needed. Stationary supply catalogs provide inexpensive, self-adhesive label holders that are easily installed and easily changed. Someone needs to be responsible for updating signs and labels for shared work materials.

Hand printed signs are OK for a day or two for staff and

customers. After that, a printed sign should be provided. Good, clear, understandable signs and labels avoid misunderstanding, frustration, and wasted time. From time to time all signs and labels will need refurbishing. Tattered, dirty, or crooked signs send the message of not caring.

Summary

Meetings may not be the answer if your primary objective is to disseminate information. You can regularly communicate through memos, e-mail, the minutes distributed from a meeting, a blog, informational binders, or a bulletin board. Putting it in writing is good for communicating with staff who like to read (visual learners). It also gives them something they can refer to when they need to double-check something or refresh their memories.

Communicating Tip #5:

Always Spell Check, Grammar Check, and Read What You Have Written.

Answer the recipients' questions–
"Why should I read this?"
"What do you want me to do?" and
"What's in it for me?"

11

Listening and Communicating as a Supervisor or Manager

Treat Your Employees as You Would Like to Be Treated

If you have any position of authority, you have the ability to not only improve your communication skills but to improve the work environment for those within your sphere of influence. Whether you are a CEO or manager, supervise only a few people, or are a team leader, you can do much to foster good communication practices in those you supervise.

Why, you may ask, should you do that? Because, not only will you have fewer personnel problems to deal with, you will have a contented and therefore productive workforce. There will be less absenteeism, less disruptive turnover, and you will have better cooperation among staff and with you. Employees who believe you care enough to listen to them will produce for you. You then will have favorable statistics to report. Once an effective communication system is set up, it takes little effort to keep it functioning, and it is well worth the time spent developing and improving it.

Effective Communicating

How do you get people to listen to you and respond to your requests? This is a common question. Answer: By using the language of power and learning to say no. Phyllis Mindell gives us some examples (55–56): While "it is true that research shows men tend not to listen to women, even when the women are their bosses. . . . It's also true that women aren't casting their directives in the language of power. Here are four directions. . . .

1. I need you to complete this report by noon.

2. So, do you think you'll get a chance to complete this report by noon?

3. If you get a few minutes, I would like you to complete this report by noon.

4. I really need this job done fast. Could you do me a favor and redesign the product?"

Now, compare that to this direction: "Please complete this report by noon." Which phrasing of the direction do you think will get the job done? (Note that using the word "please" with your direction indicates politeness but does not indicate weakness.) If you are the employee, refer back to Chapter 6 which discussed how to "Say No Powerfully but Kindly," if that is how you need to respond to such a direction.

Accessible Communicating

One of the best ways to get to know your employees is to get out of your office and walk around the plant, office, or business where your employees are working. If possible, talk to them or observe what they do. This indicates that you care enough and are curious enough to want to find out what is going on. Do not rely solely on those who report directly to you to keep you informed. Periodically check things out for yourself.

While talking to and getting to know your staff, be on the lookout for any special talents, skills, or interests an employee may have. Then use that knowledge when allocating work assignments. For example, if an employee has artistic talent or knows how to use a computer graphics program, have them do the company fliers or the in-house newsletter. This will make them feel appreciated for what they can contribute. If duties are clearly dictated in their job description, use this knowledge of your staff when working on special projects or when considering promotions.

Utilizing the Various Ways to Communicate

Try to determine their preferred way of learning. Are they visual, auditory, or kinesthetic (hands-on) learners? When training them or introducing anything new to your employees, use that knowledge to determine your approach. If you are training a group, it is best to use all three approaches. Have written instructions or handouts. Verbally go over the information in those handouts, and give your employees a chance to practice whatever you are teaching them. Use visual tools such as videos/ DVDs or demonstrations for visual learners.

Use this knowledge also when communicating one-on-one with staff. Send memos or e-mail to those who respond best to this method. Ask to speak to an individual if that works best or if there will be a lot of back and forth discussion. Always let staff try new methods/procedures before they have to implement them for customers or the public. You want to have the wrinkles ironed out before you actually put something new into play.

The employee's worksite may not be the best place to discuss complicated issues. It is therefore important to have regular staff meetings. If the group you supervise is large, then break it down into several groups and have multiple meetings. The groups should be small enough so that everyone may have a chance to speak or contribute if they need or want to. How often they occur depends on how much there is to be discussed and if time or distance is a problem. Make sure you have a good reason for the meeting. If you don't have much to discuss, make it a brief meeting or use the opportunity to get to know your staff better or to brainstorm future ideas. (A good source for solving problems in a group setting is Don Maruska's book, *How Great Decisions Get Made*.) Always follow the guidelines previously mentioned in Chapter 9—start on time; stay focused on the agenda; encourage the shy; and curtail the overly talkative. If need be, give each speaker a set amount of time. The Chair should not dominate or influence the discussions. Take care of business and adjourn.

Caring Communicating

What you should try to get across to staff is that you see them as unique individuals and that you care about what is going on at their worksite. It is a good way of averting larger problems if you are aware of what is going on and can deal with problem situations when they are still minor issues. If you know your staff, then, when they are involved in a problem situation, you will have a much better idea of how to handle it. You will know if it is something you should have the employees deal with themselves or if it is something you will need to step in and deal with.

If you know your employees, you may well know that they are capable of coming up with solutions themselves. Have staff try to work out differences rather than coming to you for a solution. However, don't assume a solution was found. There may be times when you may need to step in. Foster communication among staff by encouraging their working together respectfully. Then there will be one less thing you will have to deal with.

On the other hand, don't ignore problems hoping they will go away. They never do. Once negativity in the form of grumbling and complaining starts, it can quickly spread and infect the morale of even your best employees.

When you face employees sitting across from you in your office or in a meeting, you will need to convince them that you truly want to hear what they may have to say. They may have heard a lot of talk about how management cares about its employees. They may also have seen that in the past it was just empty rhetoric. In the past, if ideas were not well received or were ridiculed, employees may have felt reluctant to speak up. If an employee comes up with a good idea, give credit where credit is due. Staff members appreciate being acknowledged for their ideas. To not do so will shut down communication very quickly.

Effective Listening

How do you gain employee confidence and trust? Start by asking a lot of questions. Try to ask open ended questions that cannot be answered with a simple "Yes" or "No." When employees do respond, listen very carefully to what is said. Use all three types of listening outlined in Chapter 1—hearing, analyzing, and empathizing. You may need to read between the lines to interpret the feedback, since they may be afraid to speak bluntly. Realize that not all of your employees have yet developed effective communication skills.

Following through when something comes up will eventually foster trust that you mean what you say about caring and wanting their input. Back them up and/or fight for them. Of course, there may be times when that is not possible. If you cannot do it, explain why. You may have other things you need to consider when making a decision. If you explain to them why something has been handled in a certain way, they will back you up and fight for you when you need it.

Modeling Behaviors

The best thing you can do to foster good communication with your staff is to model the behaviors you want. That means do unto them what you want them to do unto you. Be honest and up-front with them. Speak your instructions or wants and needs clearly and concisely. Listen carefully and paraphrase back what you think you heard them say. Ask them for feedback on what you just said. Make very sure they understand and you are both on the same page. Do not just ask them, "Do you understand?" They will almost always say "Yes," even when they don't really understand or just "sort-of" understand.

Whether through e-mail or announcements at meetings, keep staff informed about what is going on. Even if nothing has yet been decided by management about a particular issue, rumors will fly. So keep staff in the loop by sharing what is being discussed along with the caveat that no decision has been made as yet. They may have some ideas or input that may be helpful. Help them to see the big picture and the part they play in the big scheme of things. This will help them feel that they are part of the team.

Whether verbally or in writing, always get input from staff/workgroups most affected by policy or procedural changes. They are in the best position to see where problems may occur in implementation of the changes. It is always good to have as many heads working on an issue as possible. According to James Surowiecki, author of the book, *The Wisdom of Crowds*, two or more heads are always better than one, even if that one is an expert in his field.

Courteous Communicating

Be respectful of your employees by not interrupting them in the middle of a task unless it is absolutely necessary, especially when they are engaged in an assignment that requires a great deal of concentration. Wait until they have completed that effort and then ask when would be a good time to talk. We know you are the supervisor, but this shows respect for their time and space. Interrupting their train of thought will just make the task they are doing take longer to complete. It is preferable to set up a regular meeting time with individual employees so they don't have to keep interrupting you all the time as questions come up.

If you have regularly scheduled meetings with certain staff, don't cancel (or cancel and not tell them it is canceled) unless absolutely necessary, as they may have questions that need timely answers. Give them a reschedule date and time and ask if there is anything that cannot wait until then that needs to be dealt with immediately.

Similarly, if you are going to be away from work for a long vacation, let staff know well ahead. They will appreciate the heads-up because they may need feedback from you regarding projects they are working on. It's discourteous and disrespectful to go off for a week or weeks at a time and leave staff hanging with unanswered questions. Answers to their questions will keep them productive while you are away.

Plus, with a little effort up-front to solicit ideas and freely discuss them, time and effort will not be wasted. You will avoid the situation where someone high up in the organizations gets a "brilliant" idea, implements it without getting any input or feed-back, only to find out it is unworkable and a waste of everyone's time. It pays to take the time to do it right the first time.

One-on-One Communicating

Realize that your employees have a personal life and may need time to deal with it. In these rushed, stressful times, staff need to be allowed—within reason, of course—to make personal phone calls and handle personal business during the business day. Be flexible, but set guidelines.

You can also improve communication in your workgroup by hiring good communicators for all positions. Effective communication is needed for all types of jobs. Ask in job interviews how they would respond in certain situations or ask them open-ended questions that cannot be answered with a "Yes" or "No." How they respond will give you an indication of their ability to communicate.

Another chance to do one-on-one communication with your staff is during the appraisal process. Use this as an opportunity to talk to staff informally. Give and ask for feedback (both positive and negative) from your employees. Use their comments to foster a discussion on what you see as their role in the big picture. Work with them to come up with goals that have some meaning for them and give them clear direction as to what you expect of them. According to Kenneth Blanchard and Spencer Johnson, a goal and its performance standard should be written in 250 words or less so it can be read in one minute. Make sure employees understand and agree to what you are trying to accomplish—that you have "buy-in" from them.

This appraisal discussion should not be done only once a year. This should be done on an informal basis throughout the year as different issues, especially negative ones, come up. Talking to an employee months after something praiseworthy, or in need of correction, comes up will have no value. Keep a running file of positive staff performance. Use it to provide immediate feedback and include it in their annual review. You might think of instituting a reward program to thank them for their cost-saving or efficiency-improving ideas.

Dealing with Negative and Resistant Staff

Let's first look at how negativism surfaces in a workplace and then we can explore ways to deal with it. Many agree that conditions that may bring on or increase negativity include:

- change
- unrealistic work expectations
- unclear objectives
- inadequate tools and training
- lack of control
- lack of feedback
- inadequate incentives
- physical discomfort
- lack of recognition

Change alone can create negative feelings in anyone. It can make them feel fearful, lost, resentful, doubtful, and anxious. Often when change occurs, communication spirals downward. That is precisely when it should be going up. Staff should be kept informed as to:

- what is going on
- why the change is necessary
- what it is going to entail
- what or who is going to be affected
- what new tasks or responsibilities are going to be expected of the staff

Also, this is a good time to reassure staff that you have every confidence that they can handle the change and that things may well be better after the change. However, be aware that negativity can manifest itself in subtle ways, such as:

- absenteeism

- decreased productivity

- lack of participation

- lack of cooperation

- turnover

How do you deal with negativity? Talk to your staff. Find out what the problem is. If it is one person who is causing a problem, talk to that person as suggested in Chapter 8. If it is a problem situation, see if something can be done to correct it. Again, talk to the staff. Ask them for ideas on what they would like you to do about it. Communication with your staff is the key to keeping negativity down and bringing resistors on board.

Positive Communicating

Just as negativity is contagious, so, too, is a positive attitude. You can help lift the negativity in your workplace by looking for the positive. Always keep in mind, as Blanchard and Johnson said, "The best minute I spend is the one I invest in people. . . . People who feel good about themselves produce good results." (63, 19) Therefore, try to "Catch them doing something right." (39)

Deal with negativity as soon as it shows up. Communicate with the members of your group and you will have taken a giant step toward fostering productive employees.

Summary

Treat your employees as you would like to be treated. Determine each employee's preferred way of learning—visual, auditory, or kinesthetic. Use active listening when meeting with your staff, and model the behaviors you want from them. (See Chapter 1.) Then keep them informed as to what is going on. If you are courteous and respectful to them, they will produce for you. Counter negativity with positive communication.

Communicating Tip #6:

To Foster Effective Communication, Model It with Your Staff.

Encourage staff to trust you by being trustworthy, respecting them, and backing them up when needed. Talk is cheap, so praise them whenever it is due. "Catch them doing something right."

12

Listening and Communicating as an Employee

Talk to Your Boss, Get Your Boss to Talk to You

As stated in previous chapters, the key to effective communication with another person is to try to figure out where that person is coming from and then to use that information to determine how to get them to listen to you. This approach also works when trying to communicate with your boss. Begin by trying to look at a situation or problem from the viewpoint of your boss. Then ask yourself what benefits would be achieved and how you can assist in reaching those goals. Approach your boss with the attitude of: "What can I do to help you to have a more efficient, harmonious, and, therefore, more productive department or company?" "How can we best work together on a problem or project—thereby helping us both and ultimately the whole organization?"

Determine How Your Boss Communicates (i.e., E-mail, Meetings, Never?)

Finding your boss's preference is done by listening and observing. Listen to what is said, as well as what is done (in many cases they are not the same). How does he like to communicate? Does your supervisor hole up in his office and send out a slew of e-mails or does he frequently conduct meetings? Perhaps there is never any communication with anyone about anything and therefore everyone is left guessing about what is needed or wanted. Figure out what his preferred style is and then use that to communicate with him. As John Hoover, author of *How to Work for an Idiot*, states (200):

"Every time bosses open their mouths, they are bound to provide you with valuable information about what makes them tick and what pulls their triggers. Knowledge is power."

If your boss likes to send electronic communication, send an e-mail to her regarding a problem or concern of yours. If she likes meetings, ask to have your concern put on the agenda or ask for a private meeting with her. If she prefers to discuss things in a telephone conversation, call her!

Ask Open-Ended Questions

For bosses who don't communicate with you at all, who don't give you clear directions or let you know what they expect from you, the best approach is to ask questions. After asking your question, smile and wait—as long as is necessary—until you get an answer. Ask a lot of questions if you need to. Keep asking questions until you get the response you need or you have a clear understanding of what is wanted. It is always better to ask than to guess and/or plunge ahead, and then have to redo the assignment when it turns out to be wrong.

Applying the principle of librarians from Chapter 7, possible questions you need answered by your boss are:

- What, specifically, should I be doing (first)?
- How should I be doing it?
- Am I succeeding in doing it?

- What tools and support are available?

- How does what I am doing relate to the big picture?

- How can I help you to accomplish your goals?

Persist in asking questions of your boss until you have a clear understanding. Refrain from saying, "Just what the heck is going on here?" If your boss gets impatient with so many questions, respectfully explain that you do not want to waste his/her time and yours, and that if you do not have clear indications as to what is needed or wanted, or know what the final outcome should be, you cannot do the job efficiently or effectively.

Try not to assume anything about your boss. He may be unable to express himself. Too often people end up in leadership positions who were never taught effective communication skills (not to mention management or people skills).

When approaching your boss with a problem, always bring along a possible solution.

She will appreciate not having to come up with a solution herself. Also, timing is everything. Determine the best time to approach your boss and try to do it when she is in a good mood. If you are not certain whether this is the right time or not, ask her secretary, the receptionist, or ask the boss herself.

Different Boss Types and How to Deal with Them

As mentioned in Chapter 2, different types of employees require different types of approaches to get effective results. The same holds true for bosses. The following are examples of different boss types like those in Glatthorn and Adams' book (47–48):

- The boss who doesn't consult his staff because he already knows all the answers

- The boss who is so busy networking with higher-ups he has no time for his staff

- The boss who gets defensive every time any issue is raised

- The boss who is so busy looking busy that he has no time for those he supervises

- The boss who jumps on the subordinate who brings up a problem that needs attention (and thereby discourages him from ever doing that again)

The "Good Boss" and the "Idiot Boss"

John Hoover suggests eight categories of bosses including the "Good Boss" and the "Idiot Boss." Let's look at just these two and begin with the Good Boss. Hoover (39–41) states that it is surprisingly simple to be a good boss by adopting the "... golden rule of leadership: Lead the way you like to be led." He further states:

> Good Bosses provide a constant flow of clear and concise information and encourage you and the rest of your team to do the same. Good Bosses don't like to play 20 questions in order to discern what you're talking about; they don't want to read your mind in order to learn what you're withholding; and they don't expect you to read their minds as to what they expect. . . . Good Bosses are aware that sharing information in a thorough, timely manner makes people feel included, respected, and acknowledged for their ability to contribute. They keep everybody informed all the time. And they are receptive to feedback. Not just between 3 and 4 p.m. every third Tuesday, but all of the time. It's so remarkably easy that bosses who don't do it should undergo psychiatric examination and electroshock therapy if necessary.

There should be no problem communicating with Good Bosses because they encourage staff to speak their minds.

However, according to Hoover, the one type you are more likely to encounter is the Idiot Boss. An Idiot Boss is simply chronically clueless. Try to understand his shortcomings. He may never have had any training in how to communicate or manage people. Let him see or know what you are doing because knowledge is power. This will make him feel less threatened. It is up to you to communicate with your boss and keep him informed about what you are doing. Find out from him what you should be doing and get feedback from him about your progress. If he doesn't volunteer the information, ask for it. Ask open-ended questions, offer solutions, and communicate with him in his preferred style of communication. The outcome, hopefully, will be that your boss will think well of you. As John Hoover states (181): ". . . you'll live a happier, healthier, more productive life if you develop methods and techniques to visit your . . . I-Boss's world when appropriate rather than trying to get him to visit yours."

You may think that you should not have to do all this figuring out. But we are talking about the real world and the imperfect people in it. It may not be fair, but, if you want a hassle-free workplace, it is worth the time and effort to determine how best to approach or communicate with your boss.

Remember: You Cannot Change Other People

If all efforts at understanding and working with (as opposed to for) your boss fail, you will need to decide what you are going to do. Will you be cynical or realistic? As John Hoover (239) sums it up:

> Being cynical and being realistic can appear similar in some aspects. However, being cynical engenders negativity. Being realistic is a foundation for making positive progress. Your cynical self might say, "I'm not happy about this and I don't

see it getting any better." Your realistic self will observe the same thing and say, "I'm not happy about this and the circumstances might not change anytime soon. It's time to reposition myself physically, mentally, or both to make the best of it."

As has been said before, you will have to make the decision. Will you try to achieve some understanding, give up trying and just live with it, or seek employment elsewhere? In most cases, it shouldn't come to that.

Summary

Determine how your boss communicates, then continue to ask him what he wants you to do and how well you are doing it until you have a clear understanding of what is expected of you.

Communicating Tip #7:

Ask Your Question, Smile and Wait —as Long as Necessary— until You Get an Answer.

Find your boss's preferred communication method by listening and observing—then use that to communicate with him/her.

Review

Before proceeding to Part Three, let's review the
Communicating Tips discussed in Part Two:

Communicating Tip #1:	**Choose Words That Convey Strength and Confidence.**
Communicating Tip #2:	**Practice "Customer Service" with Everyone You Deal With.**
Communicating Tip #3:	**When There Is a Problem, Deal Directly with That Person.**
Communicating Tip #4:	**Speak Clearly, Concisely, and to the Point.**
Communicating Tip #5:	**Always Spell Check, Grammar Check, and Read What You Have Written.**
Communicating Tip #6:	**(For Management) To Foster Effective Communication, Model It with Your Staff.**
Communicating Tip #7:	**(For Staff) Ask Your Question, Smile and Wait—as Long as Necessary—until You Get an Answer.**

PART THREE

"Utopia, Inc." and You!

13

A Perfect Example
at
"Utopia, Inc."

Now it's time to have some fun and put into practice what you have been reading. If you are a practical person who likes "real life" examples, this chapter will take a fairly common situation and show how a company would function if effective listening and effective communicating existed throughout the organization.

This organization, let's call it Utopia, Inc., needs to change a procedure that is not working well. Now, in most companies, procedural changes probably start with either customers' complaints, or rank and file complaining to whomever will listen about how this particular transaction or procedure is a "real pain." If it is the former, a customer will have complained to an employee, who has passed on the complaint to his supervisor. If it is the second scenario, then the employee will have reported it to her supervisor, probably after having discussed it with fellow employees to see if others have experienced the same negative occurrences or results.

Information Goes Up and Down the Ladder:

Customer Complaint—Company Response

Phase I

Let's start with the customer, whose communication was probably not in the form of "constructive criticism." The customer was probably not thinking of the betterment of the organization as a whole, but simply wanted better or faster service. The employee then made a choice as to how to respond to this complaint. The employee could have failed to listen to the complaint, or could have listened but with a nonchalant shoulder shrug, or could have simply said, "Oh well," and just ignored it.

But instead, realizing that the customer is "always" right, the employee indicated that he or she was sorry the customer was upset. Let's assume the customer was coherent and not red-faced, sputtering, swearing, or yelling. If the customer did not go into detail, the employee then proceeded to question the customer about the nature of the problem. This encouraged a dialogue and caused the customer to further communicate and to describe in more detail the nature of the problem. During this dialogue the employee was required to practice his or her superior listening skills. This might have entailed paraphrasing back to the customer what he or she had said. The customer either confirmed or corrected the employee's understanding of that dialogue—thus creating communication flow in both directions. The employee then responded to the customer that the problem would be reported, investigated, and/or corrected.

Phase II

The conversation was then reported to the employee's supervisor (who would use superior listening skills) to determine exactly where the problem lay. If it could be dealt with at that level, it was taken care of and ended there. Let's say this particular problem was not the kind of problem the employee or the supervisor could correct themselves. The supervisor then duly reported the problem to his/her supervisor at the next meeting, or followed whatever procedures were in place for communicating such information.

Phase III

Since Utopia, Inc. has such excellent communication, the CEO became aware of the problem. At the next management meeting the CEO communicated the situation to those present and asked for their input as to what their thoughts were regarding this matter. All members present gave their input with no fear that their thoughts would be ridiculed or ignored because they knew the CEO genuinely wanted to hear what they had to say. Through this open and honest discussion it was determined that the procedure should be changed.

Phase IV

Now Utopia, Inc. is such an ideal company it does not limit its discussion to top management only. An e-mail was sent to all the employees informing them that this problem had been brought to the attention of management, and asking all staff to put their creative thinking caps on, reflect on their experience in the trenches, and suggest ideas for resolving the problem.

This is an example of communication not only going up the ladder, but also information being passed down through the ranks informing everyone of the situation. Requests were then made for information to be transmitted back up the ladder so the best possible solution to the problem could be found.

All the suggestions were then gathered and discussed, either by a special committee set up to deal with the problem or at the next management meeting. By consensus, a solution or plan of action was agreed upon. Further discussion determined who would be responsible for implementing the change. That person again solicited input from all staff as to the details of how the new procedure could best be implemented (unless the original suggestion included such details). These were then distilled into a plan of action or the specifics of the new procedure.

Again we see open discussion and dialogue going up and down to the rank and file and across all departments. Since it is said that "two heads are better than one," at Utopia, Inc. management agrees: "It makes good sense to engage as many heads as possible in solving a problem."

Utilizing All Three Ways of Learning

At this point, Utopia, Inc.'s Training Department got involved in training the staff on the new procedure. Since people learn in different ways, all three ways of learning were implemented in each phase of the learning process. These training sessions included:

1. Written handouts

2. Verbal instructions

3. Hands-on practice

First, the new procedures were written out and added to the official document or manual used by the company. This also included a posting on the internal employee Intranet site. Then a training session was held for management. The Training Department or someone in the best position to do so, conducted the training sessions for staff in each department or section.

The handouts included the official written document containing the new procedure, together with instructions or suggestions (if needed) on how to implement the new procedure. The verbal instructions entailed a presentation, going over all the handouts in detail, and allowing for a question and answer period. Since many people learn best by doing, some time was also set aside for staff to practice the new procedure. Ideally, in each of the three methods of communicating the information (reading, hearing, and doing), the information was repeated at least twice. [NOTE: Studies have shown that for information to be remembered for any length of time, it must be repeated six times. This usually entails announcing what you are going to talk about, talking about it in detail, and then summarizing what you just talked about. Doing these three things, both in writing and verbally, would have the information imparted six times.]

Finally, feedback (more communication!) was requested of those taking the class to ask how well the class had been conducted. This was done on an Evaluation Form. The comments made were used to insure that relevant information was communicated successfully in future classes.

If the change was not complicated enough to require formal classes, the above information was communicated to staff via e-mail (written), or at regularly scheduled or specially held meetings (verbal), or both, with time allowed for staff to practice the new procedures (hands-on) before using them with customers. There are bound to be some questions or glitches in implementing any change, and this is best dealt with in "practice sessions," rather than in front of a customer.

Informing Customers of Procedural Changes

Utopia, Inc. was still not finished communicating about this change of procedure! Their customers needed to be informed of the change and how it might affect doing business with the company. Again, remembering the three ways people learn, the information about the new procedure was presented in written form such as signs at the company worksite, mailings to the customers, and advertisements or articles in the local paper or trade magazine. Staff verbally communicated the change to customers when they came in to do business or over the telephone when a customer called. Of course, as the procedure was being implemented, the customers (and staff) all received hands-on practice.

Even a simple change can involve a lot of written and verbal communication in order to do the job well. If a culture already exists where staff knows their input and efforts are appreciated, they will respond quickly and eagerly. This all can be done effectively without taking a huge amount of time or a huge sum of money, when all of the above communication is performed clearly and concisely.

As you can see, there is a lot of communication going on at Utopia, Inc.!

14

You Can
Achieve Success!

The importance of *listening* is the key to understanding the person you are talking with. Only through understanding that person will you know the most effective way to communicate with that person. James and Bond Wetherbe (58) state their philosophy for being a good communicator:

> ASSUME 100 PERCENT OF THE RESPONSIBILITY FOR UNDERSTANDING SOMEONE ELSE, AND ASSUME 100 PERCENT OF THE RESPONSIBILITY OF MAKING SURE THAT SOMEONE ELSE UNDERSTANDS YOU.

This means that you as the speaker have the responsibility to appeal to the listener's self-interest and communication style and thereby *motivate* the listener to want to listen to what is being said. This is almost never done and, this we believe, is why we continue to have such poor communication in so many organizations.

Practice Makes Perfect

So how can you achieve success? How can you communicate effectively at work? We recommend starting by incorporating

each of the following skills, one at a time, into your daily interaction with customers, co-workers, employees, and bosses. These
are skills that can be learned. Practice will make perfect, so start
practicing each one until it becomes part of your regular routine.
Then check it off when you have mastered it and move on to the
next one.

Checklist for Success

General

- Listen attentively, assertively, and empathetically.

- Ask open-ended questions and rephrase until you are
  sure you understand what is being said.

- Think before you speak: Who are you talking with and
  what do you want to say?

- Always answer the listener's question—WIIFM—
  "What's in it for me?"

- Be concise and to the point to help everyone save time
  and reduce stress.

Verbal

- Speak assertively, which means forcefully but without
  fear or other emotion.

- Use the active voice with a clear subject-verb-object to
  enhance understanding.

- Try to avoid "I" statements and feeling words. Trim
  hedges and slash modifiers.

- Learn to say "No" powerfully but kindly.

- Smile and be polite when talking on the telephone. Give
  the caller your full attention.

Written

- When writing, follow the same rules as verbal communication.

- All communication should follow the *Know, Feel, Do* principles—tell me what you want me to know, show me that you care, and clearly state what you want me to do.

- Be brief, respectful, and always Spell/Grammar check.

Specific

- Smile, make eye contact, and use open-handed gestures so your body language will show that you are friendly, honest, open, and caring.

- Be very organized and prepared when doing a demonstration, a presentation, or running a meeting. Have a clear idea of the main points you want to get across or agenda items that need to be addressed.

- Always start meetings on time and do not repeat what latecomers missed. If you are the Chair, keep control of the meeting and stick to the agenda.

- When speaking to any group, have written handouts, speak to them verbally, and, if possible, use some visual aid or do hands-on interactive participation.

Practice *customer service techniques* no matter who you are talking to—be they customers, co-workers, employees, or supervisors/managers. Everyone needs to feel welcome, understood, appreciated, and respected. Give them your full attention. Listen to the speaker for clues that will aid in understanding that person and what he or she is trying to say. Look to body language to enhance that understanding. Ask clarifying questions and offer solutions or alternative options. Try to give listeners what they want or need. As them, "What would satisfy you?"

Remember that the workplace today includes a very diverse group of people. Not only do we have cultural diversity, but we have different behavioral types and learning types. We also now have generational differences that affect how we view work and interact. That is why it is important to try to understand the person you are dealing with. What type of person is he, what interests her, and what would motivate him or her to want to listen to what you have to say?

Always strive to have an amicable relationship with your co-workers. There will be much less stress and more cooperation. When there is a problem, deal directly with that person. Use the FIRR technique to resolve conflict: state the facts, the impact or consequences, respect the person, and request the outcome you want to achieve. Deal with them directly, honestly, and respect-fully. Since negativity is contagious, counter it with a positive attitude, which is also contagious.

Keep in mind that while these listening and communicating techniques usually work, you cannot change other people if they cannot be persuaded to cooperate. Then you must decide if you will continue to try to achieve some understanding, give up trying and just live with it, or find employment elsewhere.

A Final Word

For *managers*, the key to establishing an atmosphere where good communication can thrive is to care about your employees. If you would like to see good productivity and thus a good bottom line, you must talk to and listen to your employees. Management should keep employees informed as to what is going on, and ask them for feedback when issues or problems are being discussed.

This can be done on a large scale throughout the organization or within small groups. Then as Blanchard and Johnson say, try to "Catch them doing something right." Praise them when they succeed.

For *everyone* in the workplace, it is essential that we all get to know each other and learn what motivates each of us to do our work—whether we are Affiliators, Power-Influencers, or Achievers. We all also need to determine our colleagues' preferred way of learning, and incorporate it into our communication with them. We all need to model the behaviors we want to see in our co-workers, employees, and bosses. This includes being honest, up-front, and respectful.

As James and Bond Wetherbe summarize (171): "Remember . . . the whole purpose of learning these techniques and developing your communication skills is to become a more effective communicator."

Paul W. Swets, author of the book *The Art of Talking So That People Will Listen* (177), states*:

> Such skills are exhilarating. Once you experience them, you will not be satisfied with anything less than your best. You will find peak communication to be positively addicting.

The two of us know from our own personal experience that the techniques we are advocating here do work! If you take each suggested step one at a time, focus on it, and practice it for a day, a week, or a month—whatever it takes until you have mastered it—you, too, will experience the exhilaration that Paul Swets refers to above. So take the first step—now, today, this minute!

* Reprinted with permission of Simon & Schuster Adult Publishing Group from *The Art of Talking So That People Will Listen* by Paul W. Swets. Copyright © 1983 by Paul W. Swets.

Will the listening

and

communicating techniques

discussed in this book

work in the real world?

Can you communicate effectively at work?

YES!

YOU CAN ACHIEVE SUCCESS!

BIBLIOGRAPHY

Barnett, Rosalind and Caryl Rivers. *Same Differences: How Gender Myths Are Hurting Our Relationships, Our Children, and Our Jobs.* New York: Basic Books, 2004.

Blanchard, Kenneth and Spencer Johnson. *The One Minute Manager.* New York: Berkley Books, 1983.

Glatthorn, Allan A. and Herbert R. Adams. *Listening Your Way to Management Success.* Glenview, IL: Scott, Foresman and Co., 1983.

Hamlin, Sonya. *How to Talk So People Listen: The Real Key to Job Success.* New York: Perennial Library, Harper & Row, 1989.

Hoover, John. *How to Work for an Idiot: Survive and Thrive without Killing Your Boss.* Franklin Lakes, NJ: Career Press, 2004.

Jensen, Bill. *The Simplicity Survival Handbook: 32 Ways to Do Less and Accomplish More.* New York: Basic Books, 2003.

Lancaster, Lynne C. and David Stillman. *When Generations Collide: Who They Are, Why They Clash, How to Solve the Generational Puzzle at Work.* New York: HarperBusiness, 2003.

Martin, William B. *Quality Customer Service.* 4th ed. Menlo Park, CA: Crisp Publications, 2000.

Maruska, Don. *How Great Decisions Get Made—10 Easy Steps for Reaching Agreement on Even the Toughest Issues.* New York: American Management Assoc., 2004.

McClelland, David C. *Human Motivation.* Cambridge, MA: Cambridge University Press, 1987.

Mindell, Phyllis. *How to Say It for Women.* New York: Prentice Hall Press, 2001.

Myers, Isabel Briggs and Peter B. Myers. *Gifts Differing: Understanding Personality Type.* Reprint ed. Palo Alto, CA: Consulting Psychologists Press, 1997.

Paul, Annie Murphy. *The Cult of Personality: How Personality Tests Are Leading Us to Miseducate Our Children, Mismanage Our Companies, and Misunderstand Ourselves.* New York: Free Press, 2004.

Solomon, Muriel. *Working with Difficult People.* Revised ed. Paramus, NJ: Prentice Hall Press, 2002.

Surowiecki, James. *The Wisdom of Crowds: Why the Many Are Smarter Than the Few and How Collective Wisdom Shapes Business, Economies, Societies, and Nations.* New York: Doubleday, 2004.

Swets, Paul W. *The Art of Talking So That People Will Listen.* New York: Fireside / Simon & Schuster, 1992.

Watson, Don. *Death Sentences: How Clichés, Weasel Words, and Management-Speak Are Strangling Public Language.* New York: Penguin Group, Inc., 2005.

Wetherbe, James C. and Bond Wetherbe. *So, What's Your Point? A Practical Guide to Learning and Applying Effective Interpersonal Communication Techniques.* Houston, TX: Mead Publishing, 2006.

ADDITIONAL READING

Adams, Scott. *The Dilbert Principle: a Cubicle's Eye View of Bosses, Meetings, Management Fads, & Other Workplace Afflictions.* New York: HarperBusiness, 1996.

Baker, Wayne E. *Networking Smart: How to Build Relationships for Personal and Organizational Success.* New York: McGraw-Hill, 1994.

Barker, Larry and Kittie Watson. *Listen Up: How to Improve Relationships, Reduce Stress, and Be More Productive by Using the Power of Listening.* New York: St. Martin's Press, 2000.

Brounstein, Marty. *Communicating Effectively for Dummies.* New York: Wiley Publishing, Inc., 2001.

Contini, Lisa. *Assert Yourself! Developing Power-packed Communication Skills to Make Your Points Clearly, Confidently, and Persuasively.* Mission, KS: SkillPath Publications, 1996.

Covey, Stephen R. *The Seven Habits of Highly Effective People: Restoring the Character Ethic.* New York: Fireside, 1990.

Frank, Milo O. *How to Get Your Point Across in 30 Seconds— or Less.* New York: Simon and Schuster, 1986.

Griffin, Jack. *How to Say It at Work: Putting Yourself Across with Power Words, Phrases, Body Language, and Communication Secrets.* Paramus, NJ: Prentice Hall, 1998.

Jensen, Bill. *Simplicity: The New Competitive Advantage in a World of More, Better, Faster.* Cambridge, MA: Perseus Books, 2000.

Jones, Barbara S. *Written Communication for Today's Manager.* New York: Chain Store Publishing Corp., 1980.

Kaumeyer, Richard A. *How to Write and Speak in Business.* New York: Van Nostrand Reinhold, 1985.

King, Larry. *How to Talk to Anyone, Anytime, Anywhere: The Secrets of Good Communication.* New York: Crown Publishers, Inc. 1994.

Krueger, Cynthia. *Hit the Ground Running: Communicate Your Way to Business Success.* St. Paul, MN: Brighton Publications, Inc., 1995.

Laborde, Genie Z. *Influencing with Integrity: Management Skills for Written Communication and Negotiation.* Palo Alto, CA: Syntony Publishing, 1983.

Lundin, William and Kathleen Lundin. *When Smart People Work for Dumb Bosses: How to Survive a Crazy and Dysfunctional Workplace.* New York: McGraw-Hill, 1998.

Morler, Edward E. *The Leadership Integrity Challenge: How to Assess and Facilitate Emotional Maturity.* Sonoma, CA: Sanai Publishing, 2005.

Morgenstern, Julie. *Making Work Work: New Strategies for Surviving and Thriving at the Office.* New York: Fireside/ Simon & Schuster, 2004.

O'Conner, Patricia T. and Stewart Kellerman. *You Send Me: Getting It Right When You Write Online.* New York: Harcourt, 2002.

O'Toole, James and Edward E. Lawler, III. *The New American Workplace.* New York: Palgrave Macmillan, 2006.

Pease, Allan and Barbara Pease. *The Definitive Book of Body Language.* New York: Bantam Books, 2004.

Plotnik, Arthur. *Spunk & Bite: A Writer's Guide to Punchier, More Engaging Language & Style.* New York: Random House, 2005.

Poley, Michelle Fairfield. *Mastering the Art of Communication: Your Keys to Developing a More Effective Personal Style.* Mission, KS: SkillPath Publications, 1995.

Richards, Dick. *Get It Across! Effective Communication at Work.* Surrey, UK: Elliot Right Way Books, 2000.

Rubin, Rhea Joyce. *Defusing the Angry Patron.* New York: Neal-Schuman Publishers, Inc., 2000.

Schwarz, Roger M. *The Skilled Facilitator: A Comprehensive Resource for Consultants, Facilitators, Managers, Trainers, and Coaches.* 2nd ed. San Francisco, CA: Jossey-Bass, 2002.

Tannen, Deborah. *Talking from 9 to 5: How Women's and Men's Conversational Styles Affect Who Gets Heard, Who Gets Credit, and What Gets Done at Work.* New York: William Morrow, 1994.

Topchik, Gary S. *Managing Workplace Negativity.* www.amanet.org: AMACOM, 2000.

Tulgan, Bruce. *Managing Generation X: How to Bring Out the Best in Young Talent.* New York: W. W. Norton & Company, 2000.

Twenge, Jean M. *Generation Me: Why Today's Young Americans Are More Confident, Assertive, Entitled—and More Miserable Than Ever Before.* New York: Free Press, 2006.

INDEX

Acknowledgments

Without the support of friends, family, and colleagues, we would not have been able to write this book. We want to acknowledge with special thanks the following for their invaluable assistance and support: Robin Hall, Cynthia Kirby, Stephanie Nicholson, Lupe Maldanado, Bill Frisch, Joan Carter, Kelly Siranko, Sheila Nemec, Michael J. Reilly, James K. Toft, Dody Anderson, and Dianne Lindgren.

Thanks are due also to our enthusiastic editor Vicki Weiland and interior designer Desta Garrett (both of whom steered us in the direction of a better book). We'd also like to acknowledge our patient cover designer Cathi Stevenson, our logo designer Sylvia Khong-Terpstra, indexer John Culleton, proofreaders Ricky Weisbroth and Marlene Michelson, and knowledgeable publicist Lin A. Lacombe.

We also give thanks for the energizing support offered by Pete Masterson and the members of BAIPA (Bay Area Independent Publisher's Association). The information we gathered and the infusion of enthusiasm we received during monthly Saturday morning meetings in San Rafael, California, have contributed greatly toward completing and publishing *Listen Up!*

ABOUT THE AUTHORS

Jane Schwamberger has experienced both highly successful communication and poor communication in her varied positions in the states of New York, Florida, Washington, and California. She has worked at the McGraw-Hill Publishing Company in New York City and in retail on Long Island (NY). Most of her experience is in libraries, where she has held a variety of positions, including Reference Librarian, Director of Children's Services, Library Director in Florida, Branch Manager in Florida and Washington State, Consultant and Training Librarian in California. While Director of the New Port Richey Public Library (FL), she implemented a highly successful communication program with her staff, city staff, library board members, community agencies, and Friends of the Library. Throughout her career, she has been aware of the need for improved communication practices and has actively developed and implemented them. As the Training Librarian for Santa Cruz Public Libraries (CA) she began working with Eunice LeMay, who became her assistant in 1999. Their experience of excellent communication with each other led to the desire to work together on projects that would share effective communication techniques with others.

Eunice LeMay has held numerous positions throughout her working life, ranging from a customer service job as a Big Boy hostess, to factory work pressing pants at Jack Winter, to ten years in the Funds Transfer Department at a Wisconsin bank. After moving to California in 1985, she was a Unix Systems Administrator at a small Information Technology company and volunteered at a library where, among other things, she taught Internet classes to the public. When working with her boss (Jane Schwamberger) as the Assistant to the Training Librarian, she realized the importance of good communication in the workplace, which led to the increasing desire to teach others about the benefits of good communication. In addition to teaching Internet classes to the public, she has taught elementary school. Most recently she taught several of the new employee training classes at Santa Cruz Public Libraries (CA), and she has also used her communication knowledge in her position as a Branch Manager there. Now she and Jane are sharing their discoveries about effective communication through seminars and speaking engagements.

Contact Information

Submit Examples

We welcome your feedback!
To contact us or submit examples of poor or excellent communication, visit our website:

www.papiliopublishing.com

Send mail to: Papilio Publishing
                   P.O. Box 4197
                   Santa Cruz, CA, 95063-4197

Send e-mail to: JaneS@papiliopublishing.com

                   EuniceL@papiliopublishing.com

Seminars, Workshops, and Speaking Engagements

Contact us as at:

trainings@papiliopublishing.com

Buy the Book

If you enjoyed this book, and would like to order additional copies for yourself or for friends, please check with your local bookstore, favorite online bookseller, Amazon, Baker & Taylor, or place your order directly with the publisher.